Macalister
or
Dying in the Dark

Other Books by Douglas LePan

POETRY

The Wounded Prince
The Net and the Sword
Something Still to Find
Weathering It
Far Voyages

FICTION

The Deserter

MEMOIRS

Bright Glass of Memory

Macalister
or
Dying in the Dark

a fiction based on what is known of his life and fate

by **Douglas LePan**

Quarry Press

Copyright © Douglas LePan, 1995.

All rights reserved.

The publisher gratefully acknowledges the support of
The Canada Council, the Ontario Arts Council,
the Department of Canadian Heritage,
and the Ontario Publishing Centre.

Cataloguing in Publication Data

LePan, Douglas, 1914—
   Macalister, or Dying in the dark

Verse drama.
ISBN 1-55082-139-3

   I. Title.   II. Title: Dying in the dark.

PS8523.E67M33   1995   C812'.54   C95-900161-1
PR9199.3.L45M33   1995

Cover art entitled "Warrior and Shield" (1953-54), a bronze by Henry Moore,
reproduced by permission of the Art Gallery of Ontario.

Design by Susan Hannah.
Typeset by Chris McDonell.

Printed and bound in Canada
by Tri-Graphic, Ottawa, Ontario.

Published by Quarry Press, Inc.,
P.O. Box 1061, Kingston, Ontario K7L 4Y5.

*Dedicated to Madame Jeannine Macalister
in memory of her husband*
JOHN KENNETH MACALISTER
*born in Guelph, Ontario, Canada, July 1914
executed at Buchenwald, September 1944*

Shemà
You who live secure
In your warm houses,
Who return at evening to find
Hot food and friendly faces...

Primo Levi
10 January 1946

Dramatis Personae

The protagonist, JOHN KENNETH MACALISTER — *hero, anti-hero, and victim*
His wife, JEANNINE MACALISTER
His mother, MRS. A. M. MACALISTER
The author (who is also questioner, double, and poet)
A military historian
A scattering of other voices

One

Invocation by his double, who is also a contemporary and compatriot

Speak to me

you who have haunted me so long
with your sad brown eyes and your terrible fate
    (on a meat-hook! on a meat-hook!)
whose life for so long was so like mine but then took
a turn that led irreparably into the dark . . .

It was a few days after the uneasy peace. A bright
spring sun was skirling the pigeons up into the air
round Nelson's column and Landseer's lions. The fountains
were frolic. And I was too, in spite of the millions dead,
glad to be alive, in spite of the dead and the new troubles
sprouting in the dark of the red boxes round my desk,
despatches from Moscow, Warsaw, Paris — trouble!
Then I put in my key and, opening another box,
first learned what had happened to you (and Frank Pickersgill)
at Blois, on the Avenue Foch, at Fresnes, and at Buchenwald
    (on a meat-hook! on a meat-hook!)
All that in the cool clear prose of the Foreign Office. I knew then
a hook had gone into my gills that would never come out . . .
Years later when I was guiding the College where we both
were students (did we ever meet? I don't think so)
your eye would catch mine in the gloom of a November corridor

or a grim gargoyle would be transformed into your broad
open candid face, as I was hurrying to a Council meeting.
A better man than I was, I always knew, and braver,
far braver, yet so like me in other ways, my ghostly double
to remind me of the ghastly way we've come. Before I left
I'd saved a demilune of grass behind the College for you
in the hope that someday there would be a sculpture there
as your memorial. But that's still to do. And now light thickens
as I strive to quicken another kind of breathing bronze
and bring quivering to the light
                                          your agony in the dark.
But how am I to tell your story without your help
whose lips were closed so long ago, who left so little?
So speak to me, speak.

Now there are voices. But other voices, women's voices.

His wife speaks

      And speak to me, your wife, who still bears your name
and bore your child, your still-born child, that the war
tore from me. I think of it as a black whirlwind
that tore my husband from me, and my child, my father too —
round the world a black whirlwind blowing from pole to pole
from the South Sea islands to the Arctic ice-floes
and not least over torn divided France, defeated, shamed,
which seemed then all the world to me, or almost.
I was so young and innocent then, we both were,
in our different ways. We never thought that France
could fall, and fall so quickly. Our love would make
catastrophe impossible. And so you went sadly back to England.
Then that June the German panzers churning the *terre sainte*
of fair fertile France, the tens of thousands killed,
the millions taken prisoner, the millions on the roads,
homeless and hopeless, not knowing where to go

> (How many tears our Blessed Mother Mary must had shed,
> Mary, Mother and Virgin!)

carrying a few pitiful belongings, sheltering in ditches,
pouring into Lisieux and beyond, on into Brittany.
And then the German soldiers, some of their officers even
in our own house, all of them so correct, punctilious,
we never could have dreamt . . . Those long years
when I never heard, or heard so little, a card or two
through Tunis or Tangier, and that was all. Until . . .
oh your tender neck, so firm, so tender, as I would clasp it
when we were making love, your lips to mine, your thighs to mine.
So speak to me, speak.

His mother speaks

And speak to me, your mother, who heard much less.
I was never even told the way my own son died,
was never allowed to know, though others knew,
it showed too plainly in their faces. And then they wondered
why I wouldn't talk of you, why I'd sit silent
as though I wouldn't, couldn't, accept your death.
I didn't want to hear their talk, their voices — only yours,
so soft and strong, and then (when you were pleased, amused,
or merely playful) ending in a little upward "Ah" —
almost falsetto. Even as a little boy you talked like that,
when you were having trouble buttoning the dickey
in your sailor suit and would call for me, or later,
when you would talk to me of school or college and tell
me of your triumphs — although you never made them seem
like triumphs — in class or on the rugby field or in debates.
I gave you up. First to Toronto where first your star
began to shine, and then to Oxford where it shone more brightly.
I gave you up, a mother's fatal, necessary gift.
Always you were gentle and affectionate, to me and others,
but firm, determined, conscious of your own worth
and of the duties it imposed. But were you conscious

of the high-strung nerves behind your eagerness and ardour?
Were those who chose you as a secret agent? Were those who sent you?
Only a mother knows such things about the child she bore.
Only a mother knows what grief it is to lose an only son.

Again his double speaks
>It's late
>
>and so few things of yours are left
>to help give credence, breathing, cadence to your story,
>a photograph or two, perhaps a dozen letters,
>shards that I've hunted high and low for.
>
>And those who knew you? Some long gone to the farther shore,
>some now easily forgetful, or with their wits stained by dementia,
>only a very few who remember you as you were, and as
>I've come to know you, someone who won all the prizes
>yet whom everybody liked, who was everyone's "best friend"
>because you cared about so many. That's how I see you still,
>I who have no claim on you as either kin or comrade
>yet feel consanguined in a strange complicity that drives
>me on to tell your story.
>
>It's late. So speak to me, speak.

After a long pause he appears
>I was dreaming, dreaming of one fall morning in Guelph.
>(Did you know I was "a dreamy thoughtful guy"?
>That's what one girl called me. I was irritated at the time,
>but it was true, I guess.) In just one night a maple tree
>in the park across the road from us had lost all its leaves
>and they lay crisped and curled in a kind of papery froth
>that was inches thick, a bright thick froth of red and white,
>the red upper sides of the leaves and their white undersides
>though the red was not quite red, but more like blood spilt

on a not too clean surface, and the white was not quite white
but more the color of flesh when it's almost drained of blood.

A naked tree. A bright brave froth of fallen leaves. I knew
it couldn't last. In a night or two a heavy rain would wash
the blazoning off and leave underfoot a sodden mass.
But that morning it had its moment, as I watched
the early sun slice through the trees . . . like a moment in man's
life . . . or a nation's . . . before time sluices it away.

Then more guardedly
    — But whom am I speaking to? Who was it called me?
    — A friend, who only wants to ask you a few questions.
    — I am wary of questions. They can be dangerous, treacherous.
    — But mine are friendly. Not at all dangerous or treacherous.
    — Perhaps. Do you know what *question* can mean in French?
    — I think so. I'm not sure, though, I remember. So tell me.
    — Torture. Interrogation of a prisoner. Torture.
    — Perhaps I should let you finish what you were dreaming.

He goes on, as his double enters the shadows
    That was the park I played in as a child, where later
I would take my books to study on warm spring afternoons,
where I would walk my girl-friends. A little paradise.
In winter the purple shadows slanting on the snow,
and I'm in snow-shoes — imagining myself a brave out hunting —
but actually a clumsy oaf whenever from sheer vanity
I'd take my glasses off, falling over my own feet,
an untried youth who sometimes dreamt of some great test . . .

Now dreamy summer's back and through the foliage
I see twin towers — of stone, I think? yes, stone — towers
rising to Our Lady, cathedral-like, but not rising from
a level square, like Notre Dame in Paris, but rising from
a hill — the Catholic Church that centres the green city

of my childhood. I'm there taking my first Communion,
and that's me near the altar serving as a surpliced altar-boy,
    (So many towers that I've been called to! And then
      that final summons, to the dark tower,
        "*Achtung! Achtung!*")
I went first with my mother, and later went to please her,
long after I was certain whether I believed or not.
My father never came. Long since he'd ceased believing,
as he and my mother had long since fallen out of love,
although they both loved me, as parents will an only child . . .

Now twin towers merge in one, not Gothic now, but Norman
(if you could call it that), the Norman keep of the College[1]
where I went, four-square against the winds and years,
"godless" as it was called, but dear to me and full of grace
as any house that claims a more direct divine descent.
I'm climbing now. It must be up the winding stair
that leads to the open platform at the top that then
looked out over a tranquil and still-full-foliaged Toronto.
    (to the dark tower, "*Achtung! Achtung!*"
      those words re-echoing)
And climbing, too, to the height of my own mind. For the first time
up those draughty stairs to "What is real?" "How can we know?"
"What is it makes us human?" "What are the grounds of right and wrong?"
And the grounds of law, particular and universal, that *jus gentium*,
the firm foundation of a civil polity, in nations and among them.
I'm dreaming, though. Were those all figments of a dream-world, too?
    ("*Achtung! Achtung!*"
      and the door clangs shut.)

Two

His questioner moves half-way out of the shadows

— But what was it took you to where the door clanged shut?
That's what I'm wondering, it seems so out of character,
so out of keeping with everything we know about you,
a gentle unassuming nature, an academic record far better
than mine — mine wasn't bad — an air almost of diffidence.
— There were so many doors. I hardly know how to answer.
(with more spirit, almost irritably)
But who are you to claim to know my character, my nature?
Who are you, anyway?
— I'll move a little more into the light. Perhaps that will help.
— All I can see hazily is a figure glimpsed a few times
in a corridor or at a meeting. We spoke perhaps once or twice.
Douglas, I think. I remember then you had a troubling stammer.
— And you were Kenneth. At least to your friends and family.
So why in the British Army were you nearly always John?
— It didn't seem to matter. When I'd joined the training depot
I'd fallen so far down I'd lost myself, was how it seemed.
That endless polishing of buttons, buckles, boots.
That endless Guards' drill — stomping it out in the grey parade-ground
in the grey gun-metal light, right turn, left turn, about turn,
to the bark of a hectoring sergeant. My muscles hardened. I stood
up straighter. But was there still an "I"? I often doubted it,
so why bother worrying about what they called me, John,
or Ken, or Kenneth, or whatever. Then when I moved on

and was in training as an agent, neither of my christening names
seemed valid. I had as many aliases as a pick-pocket.
My code name, field name, cover name. Those were the names
I had to cling to. A cleverly designed disguise to enter into —
with a new identity card, and ration card, and travel permit
all properly sealed
      and signed
           and countersigned.
     They now were me.
— But I'm still wondering how you got to where the gates clanged shut.
— And I now can see you're not a very skilled interrogator.
They never ask the crucial question first, but wait
until they've worn the prisoner out with a multiplicity
of minor things. And then they pounce. And then if they're
not satisfied, in come the SS with their fists and truncheons.
— As you like. Let's move a little further back, then.
I don't even understand why you joined the British Army.
— The Canadian Army wouldn't have me. I was too short-sighted.
— That's what they told me, too. Later they weren't so choosy.
— I couldn't stay in wartime Oxford. With my wife in France
how could I go back to Canada? What would you have done?
— I know. I sympathize. In '39 and '40 I had my own
dilemmas that were not all that different from yours,
I thought the war had to be fought. But it took me a long time
before I managed to be enlisted in the field artillery.
— I agreed the war had to be fought. But what was I to do?
I didn't want to hide my light entirely under a bushel.
I'd come back to Oxford to finish my training as a lawyer,
but, as I was writing my last law examinations, dive-bombers
were strafing the last soldiers on the beach at Dunkirk.
Two weeks later I applied to join the Field Security Police.

The voice of a historian from the wings
  That means nothing to you? Then, as a military historian, I'll try to clue
  you in. On the outbreak of war in '39, the Field Security Police was

set up to guard against enemy spies and saboteurs behind the lines or, in the jargon of the day, to guard against the Fifth Columnists who had played such a part in the demonology of the Spanish Civil War. To man its ranks, the War Office advertised for personnel with special qualifications, particularly in languages, and they flowed in, a motley crew, mostly of intellectuals of every kind who had some skill in languages. For administrative purposes, though, the new service was lumped in with the Corps of Military Police, the "Red Caps", known and feared not only by deserters but by every soldier who had overstayed his leave. So brain and brawn bunked down more or less together, an odd couple, to be sure. Hence the Guards' drill and the endless spit and polish at the training depot. But after basic training, they went their separate ways, and in the winter of '41 three Field Security Sections were assigned to oversee security at the training schools for secret agents run by SOE.

That's another story, the story of SOE, the Special Operations Executive. But perhaps now is as good a time as any to fill you in on that as well.

After France surrendered, how was the war to be won? By blockade? bombing? Britain stood alone, remember, as we've been told so often, although that's a little cavalier about the other nations in the Commonwealth, including Canada. In Whitehall the Cabinet and the planners still told themselves it could be done. But how? Partly out of delusion and partly out of desperation they added sabotage and subversion to bombing and blockade and set up SOE to foment resistance and to run secret agents into occupied Europe. Their role would not only be sabotage and subversion but also to train and equip resistance networks that would come fully into their own when the time came to invade. So in July 1940 SOE was established as an organization quite separate from the Secret Service, MI-6, whose role was espionage abroad, and from MI-5, whose role was counter-espionage at home, and given its charter with Churchill's words, "And now set Europe ablaze!" Beyond a tiny few, no one was even supposed to know of its existence. Its headquarters were in Baker

Street, and by those few in the know, it was often referred to merely as
"Baker Street" or, even more cryptically, simply as "the Organization".

His questioner and double continues
— So in September you enlisted in the Field Security Police —
but not without some hesitation, I would gather.
— *(Startled, irritated)* Where did you learn that?
— I guessed it. From some papers that have come my way.
— Well, it's true. And it has some bearing on my story later.
I'll tell you why. But not before you tell me why *you*
enlisted when the issues seemed to others far from clear
and when you had so many other options open to you.
This questioning, you know, is a game that two can play at.
— Down a long tunnel
                          darkly
or down the rifling of a rifle-barrel
                                        that's how those years
seemed to me then, still seem to me now.
One darkness after another, with little light in between,
one aggression after another and not much done
about any of them. The air a babble of voices —
communists, pacifists, isolationists, realists, idealists,
and disillusioned idealists who argued for doing nothing.
And all the time (for me at least) a dark stain spreading —
what Hitler was doing to the Jews, boycotts, beatings by
the Brownshirts and later by the Blackshirts (while the police
stood idly by), purges of doctors, lawyers, bureaucrats,
mixed marriages forbidden, the Jews no longer even citizens.
I soon knew in my own mind that Hitler had to be defeated.
There were ambiguities, yes, but one growing certainty
however clouded by the witness of misguided prophets.
            (A long dark tunnel
                          rifled with circling arguments.)
What then to do? I admit I had one clear advantage

over others to whom the Nazis seemed a long, long way away.
I was in Europe for a student conference in June of '34
when Hitler flew to Munich, arrested the leaders of the Brownshirts
and had them shot out of hand, without arraignment, trial or
defence, while on his orders Goering in Berlin was doing the same
to Schleicher, Strasser, and to others who were leaders in Catholic Action.
"I was the sole justiciar of the German people that day," so Hitler said.
I knew then that a once-great nation was in the hands of thugs and gangsters.
— They seemed the same to me those years, but different too.
     High in the air
              two birds coupling
              in storm in tempest
        the whirlwind stained by scarlet droplets of delight.
That's what I see most of all.
                But what of Jeannine?
How can I tell how it still seems to her, our coming together,
our coupling, as the war was starting? There in a niche of Normandy
where the fields and orchards were lush, seemed fat as butter,
seemed to be running over with cream and calvados.
When I was captured, it was her plight I worried about
almost as desperately as I did about my own,
about how she might be forced, because of me,
one day to peer down, down into the eye of the abyss.
But that was later. At first it was all lightness, happiness.
So that's why the 'thirties were the same for me, but different,
a long dark threatening tunnel, a long bleak winter,
but at the end a sense of lightness, of life returning,
the sense you have in Toronto when you hear the gulls again
in early March.
           Slower than you, to know the war had to be fought,
and slower than you, to know the nature of the Nazis,
but that perhaps for reasons good as well as bad.
I felt obliged to follow carefully the arguments
of the "false prophets", as you call them, the appeasers and isolationists,
partly because they might be right — although I doubted that —

but more because I could hardly bear to see the few flimsy
filaments of order that still held the world together sacrificed
in a maelstrom that almost anyone could see would swirl world-wide.
So as one act of aggression followed another, I sheltered
more or less with those who acquiesced in what was done —
and not done — in Abyssinia, Spain, the Rhineland, Austria,
the Sudentenland, although feeling more and more foreboding,
even sometimes something like a sense of guilt — or shame.
Perhaps you might think a Catholic boy should have been alert
to catch a whiff of sheer depravity, to catch the stench of evil.
But others whom I thought my betters were just as slow as I was,
and by then I stood at quite some distance from the catechism,
from the quick certainties about right and wrong that I'd been taught.
At last the balance tipped, though.
                              — Was that because of Munich?
— No, it was after that. One day I saw a newsreel
of a Nazi rally, and there was Streicher, the author of all that filth
about the Jews, standing at Hitler's right. And that pointed
deeper than I'd ever pierced before into the black heart of Nazi-ism
and showed anti-semitism standing close to its very core.
I knew then what a vile regime it was.
                              — As I did, too.
And knew it had to be defeated.
                              — As I did, too,
and knew it had to be defeated, even if it cost all of us our lives.
I couldn't sleep then. My law-books lay unopened,
Gaius and Grotius, the historians of the common law,
the civil law with its various exegetes and codifiers.
Somehow I saw our civic polity stripped of its sophistications,
stripped to a beating heart, a simple courage, that pumped
its lifeblood through our puny efforts at comity and justice.
And saw myself stripped of my ambitions and aspirations,
stripped to something much more simple and afraid, wondering
what I would be willing to die for, and in that wonder
somehow forgetting fear and gaining a strange new sense of being,

of coming to be. It was that awe that kept me sleepless
night after night, unable to study, unable to smell spring
coming on in Oxford. But my body was too strong and healthy
for me to stay that way for long, thinking about me thinking,
about me being, about my essence and my finiteness. Soon
I was reading and taking notes again, and playing tennis, and planning
for the future, preparing to enter law and public life
in Canada. For that I'd need a better grasp of French.
So late that spring I'm back in France and living with a family.

Three

He glides away, the light changes, and after a few moments he returns

>High in the air
>>two birds coupling
>>in storm in tempest
>the whirlwind stained by scarlet droplets of delight
>The cry of gulls.
>>The ravenous cry of life, of spring, of strength.
>And add to that (as a few weeks afterwards in Guelph or in Toronto
>is added the song of robins, sweetest of songs from one of the commonest
>of birds) the cry of sweetness. I'm in her arms again
>treading out a measure of strength and sweetness interlinked,
>entering her ever more deeply, as she holds me, clings to me.
>Why shouldn't we marry? The war may soon be over.
>It's still unreal, this *drôle de guerre,* this long strange lull
>behind a Line that's thought impregnable. And if storm follows
>what better defiance to the whirlwind than out of joy and love
>to form another being? What better answer to the gulls' scream
>and the robins' descant from the tall nearby tree?
>>Or is that sophistry?
>And I more bound by her naked beauty, by sensual ecstasy?
>Is that what keeps me here, smoking one Gauloise after another,
>as telegrams call all Rhodes Scholars back to Oxford?

His wife, to one side of him
>Even lying in his arms, I know he's troubled.

I know he's torn apart because of me.
There's worry in his sweat, and indecision,
a deep restlessness in his limbs as well as love.
I've told him he should do as he thinks best
even if that should take him back to England
or, farther still, to Canada. At that
he shakes his head, but looks undecided
and goes outside and walks among the pear-trees
but soon comes back in and lights another cigarette.
Yesterday he went to Caën and tried to join
a unit in the French Army as a volunteer.
I told him that was folly, but he had to find
out for himself. As he did, of course. They wouldn't
take him: first, he wasn't French and, then
— how do you say? — his eyes were too myopic.
That night there were two letters waiting for him,
one from his professor, calling him back to Oxford,
and another from his mother calling him home
to Canada. And me? I'm so torn too.
He is my husband and my lover. No, more than that,
my world, a world I hardly knew existed.
But how can I leave my family, my father, mother,
with France at war, and my father old and ill?

His mother, to the other side of him
    So far away. It's all so far away.
    And I'm so much alone. I climb the steps
    of our Church here to Mary the Immaculate
    and light a candle praying for my dear, dear son.
    Who does not know a mother who has lost her husband's love
    and turns instead for comfort to her son
    and invests in him what's left of all her hope
    although she knows that she must give him up
    at last to others, to his wife, his work, his fate?
    Who does not know a mother who finds it hard

to make that sacrifice, but prepares himself
to welcome her new daughter with joy and kindness?
But when it's all so far away
      and in another country
            and in another tongue?
Mary, mother of Jesus, pray for her, pray for me,
and pray for us all in our troubles, our perplexities.

He resumes, while his wife and mother remain on each side of him, half in shadow
 So I went back to Oxford, leaving my wife in Normandy,
sad, sick at heart, but knowing why she couldn't follow me.
The salt sting of winter spindrift as I crossed the Channel.
I wouldn't go inside. The cold seemed more companionable.
Walking the deck, round and round, as Le Havre fell far behind
and England still was wrapped in fog.
           A chasm opening.
A darkened firth.
     But *(angrily)* you don't understand?
Or find it incomprehensible? My leaving her? Or her not following?
Or both? What do you know of wartime partings, separations?
And if they're too much for you, how do you ever hope
to know the way we've come, the world we've lived in?

Well, *(more quietly now)* on that channel crossing a vague sense deepened
of a fork in the road, of roads dividing — and the signs all down —
of going into an unknown where a man could be called to walk
two roads at once (with his crotch impaled on the forking road,
threatening to tear him apart), so much so that when I came down
the gangway at Southhampton and felt the jetty heave beneath me
my head was reeling to the point of vertigo, reeling far more
than from the Channel chop. And it was even worse at Easter
when I made the trip again to Normandy to see Jeannine,
who then was three-months pregnant. And then in May and June
the Blitzkrieg — and the panzer columns slicing deep inside France.

His mother speaks
>I pleaded with him then, pleaded with all my might
>in letter after letter, that he come home to Canada
>where he could do whatever he thought to be his duty
>just as well as he ever could in England.
>   And, goodness gracious me!
>he'd volunteered for the French Army and been rejected,
>and volunteered for the Canadian Army and been rejected,
>and even the British wouldn't take him as an ordinary soldier,
>he was so short-sighted, but only for some special service,
>as he explained it to me. His wife was still in France,
>I know. But what good could he do her by staying on
>in England that he couldn't do just as well in Canada
>now that Europe was a German fortress, and bolted, barred?
>As I sat at my little desk by the window, writing him
>my heart was pounding. Was I to blame for mentioning
>in my letters the warning of those palpitations?

His wife speaks
>I didn't plead. I couldn't. But I didn't need to.
>His heart was locked in mine, and mine in his.
>Without that certainty, I never could have stood
>my pregnancy. Morning after morning
>I felt so sick. But I never knew whether it was
>a natural sickness from the child that I was bearing,
>or nausea because of Kenneth's absence from me,
>or a deep despair that came from France's overthrow.
>As the day wore on, though, my mood would often lighten.
>My horizon would open, brighten. Perhaps the war
>would end, and end in victory. Perhaps my husband
>would be restored to me in all his handsome, lissom
>strength, that could always turn girls' heads, like mine.
>I'd go out and walk a half-hour in our rose-garden,
>dreaming among the butterflies, among the summery
>airs and fragrances, and summoning back

> the serious calm that seemed so natural to him
> — but with little rippling gusts of playfulness —
> still thinking of his clear brown eyes, his dark brown hair,
> and all the while holding him, holding him fast to me.

He comes forward a little from between his mother and his wife
> You see how I was torn. And it showed in how I acted,
> I'm afraid.

His double materializes to one side and looks at him questioningly
> No, there are some things that I'd rather have others tell.

The voice of a military historian from the wings, as his wife and mother fade from view
> Our records show that late in May of 1940 — I don't know the exact date — John Kenneth Macalister applied to be enlisted in the Field Security Wing of the British Intelligence Corps. On July the 1st he was interviewed and accepted, subject to the usual checks and investigations, and told that he would probably be called for enlistment at the end of the month. Then there was delay, which led to a strange sequence of events, that shows how deeply he was torn and troubled.
>
> On August the 8th he wrote to the recruiting officer for the Field Security Police asking that his application be withdrawn, and two days later he was informed by letter that his request had been granted. So much is clear. What follows is, in some places, hazy and, in other places, bizarre. But it appears that on September the 4th, at his request, the Warden of Rhodes House wrote to the headquarters of the Field Security Police in London, explaining his predicament (now that his Rhodes Scholarship had run out, leaving him without anything to live on in England) and requesting that his recruitment be expedited. A few days later the military authorities replied with scarcely veiled astonishment, since they had taken him at his word and cancelled his application. But if he had changed his mind again, as they put it, they promised to send him recruiting authority, so that he could be enlisted immediately. That was done, and he was formally attested into the British Army shortly

after the middle of September of 1940 — again I am unsure of the exact date.

    The to-ing and fro-ing was not yet over, however. At about the same time, apparently, he had received a very attractive offer from the University of Toronto of a lectureship in the Department of Law there, and his parents not unnaturally hoped that he would accept. The irresolution this caused culminated in something almost farcical. Taking up the cudgels on his behalf, his landlady in Oxford got on the telephone to the War Office in London and to the Field Security training depot in Winchester in a passionate but vain attempt to have his enlistment rescinded. She failed, of course. The same day he finally arrived at the depot in Winchester.

He comments and continues
    Yes, that's true. All of it.

    But there's worse, that you might as well hear from me
    as from some papers you might stumble on.
    Between applying for enlistment and actually enlisting
    I booked passage on a ship to Canada, in August.
    Would I really have sailed away from England that summer
    when everything seemed to hang trembling in the balance?
    I don't know. *(He hangs his head.)* I somehow doubt it, now.
    But who can ever know the answer to that kind of question?
    Who ever really knows why he acted as he did?
    Yet there it is. I'd applied to join the British Army
    and then put down my name for a sailing back to Canada.
        A silly yo-yo that a kid might play with
            up
                                    and then up again.
            and then down

His double intervenes
    Aren't you being too hard on yourself? It's a summer
    I remember well. Decisions weren't all that easy.

Impatiently, brushing aside possible excuses
    And poor Mrs. Stott, my landlady. Hiding behind her skirts.
    Letting her 'phone the War Office and the O.C. down in Winchester.
        Yes, a yo-yo
                up
                                      and up again
            and then down

Again his double and defender breaks in
    You couldn't stay in Oxford. I was at Harvard then
    and felt I couldn't stay there either, with the air blue
    from controversy between isolationists and interventionists
    and I must keep my mouth shut as an alien on a visa.
    I'd canvassed all the services in Canada
    and I canvassed them again. No, they wouldn't have me,
    I wasn't needed. At last I remember saying to myself
    "To hell with it! I'll go to Mexico and write the book
    that I've been trying to write". Of course I didn't go.
    The next year saw me on a troopship bound for England.
    But my indecisions were at least as bad as yours, or worse,
    the waverings of a self-important pinchbeck Hamlet.

Hardly having heard, but calmer now, he starts on another stage of his journey
    It was only on the train to Winchester that my head began to clear.
    Had I been on the brink of breakdown? I think I must have been.
    The wheels were comforting. I was dozing off a little . . .

    to come up against a strength, a firmness, a kind of cable
    where my heart should be,
    a cable twisted of dim, past fortitudes and resolutions,
    some older than myself, woven by my Highland forebears,
    some by my parents' care for me, some by my wife's fearless love,
    but some of my own making, from all those hours
    I'd spent thinking about the grounds of right and wrong
    in a man's life and (more difficult) in nations and among them,

and from thinking . . . no, something more and less than thinking . . .
from the pure play of spirit in those sacred clearings
where I had known, where I had seen, what I would die for,
moments too pure to last, but always there to be revived.
It was those moments now that spoke to me, strengthening me,
making me half-forgive myself for all my indecisions.
My mind was a sheer transparency as I recognized their source:
an over-fondness of myself as someone special,
an over-estimation of my worth and my achievements,
(an Oxford double first isn't quite a Nobel Prize)[2]
an ambition that may have been too personal and possessive.
But wasn't everyone of worth, and special to some eyes?
Wasn't everyone of worth to God, and at least special there?
And hadn't it been made crystal-clear to me what must be done?
Now it was for me to take my share of that coarse burden.
And never again could there be any turning back.

Four

As he subsides into the shadows, there is a scatter of voices from a number of points off-stage, interspersed with faint bugle-calls in the distance

> "He looks on his work as a mission from which nothing will be allowed to divert him . . . resourceful and full of stamina."

> "Security-mindedness is ingrained in this student, who is quiet and reserved . . . but with plenty of acumen and savoir-faire."

> "His appearance is deceptive. He gives the impression of easy-going urbanity, while in reality he has a particularly tough scholar's mind, logical and uncompromising in analysis."

> "He sees the Nazi menace as a cancer which calls for drastic surgery and consequent willingness for sacrifice on the part of those who are to be the instruments of it."

The voices and bugle-calls fade away, and he and his questioner again emerge from the shadows
— Do those comments sound at all familiar to you?
— Not very. Perhaps a little like some of the clichés
that reporting officers write about an agent
after he's finished one sequence of his training
and he's moving on — to another school in the Highlands,
say, for commando training, or to Ringway, or Grendon
Underwood, the wireless school, or Beaulieu Abbey.[3]

— Clichés? They don't seem very cliché-like to me
they're too focused, too personal, too particular.
And you should know the particular agent they refer to.
It happens to be you.
     — I can't believe it.
Those comments could only apply to one of the real stars
of SOE, to someone decisive and severe like Francis Cammaerts
or to someone decisive and exuberant like Harry Rée,
both of whom I knew well and liked, admired,
but whom I knew that I could never hope to emulate.
 (Doubt entering
 like frost in masonry
doubt whether I was ever cut out to be a secret agent.
That was the question that I lived with day by day
as I was going through the training schools.
 Doubt entering
 like frost in masonry
 day after day, deeper and deeper
 and the daily effort to combat it.)
No, I can't believe it. There must be some mistake.
Those comments couldn't possibly refer to me.
— There's no mistake. The reports are there in black
and white in archives in the Foreign Office, reports
on your performance after you'd taken the leap,
and applied to leave the Field Security Police,
and been accepted for training as a secret agent.
— The reporting officers were too easily hoodwinked, then.
But I'll admit I gave the courses all I had.
Often when I was growing up in Guelph,
and playing rugby, I'd be given the ball and told
to plunge head-first and hell-for-leather through
the line, using my strength and stubbornness in place
of the finesse I didn't have without my glasses.
I'd sometimes think of that when I was trying to use heart
to cover my lack of skill in subterfuge and deceit

— or perhaps it was lack of nerve, I'm not sure which —
as I was learning codes and ciphering, and unarmed combat,
and how to frustrate even a tough interrogator.
But those reports that you've let me hear, were they
the only comments on my performance? I seem to remember
being ticked off for nerve-storms, brain-storms, and told
that they would be entered in my dossier. And earlier
still, while I was a small cog in Field Security, before
I'd joined the Organization, I was put up for a commission
and interviewed and turned down flat, the reason being,
so I was told, that the panel found me "too diffident."
— Yes, all those facts are in your file. They hardly count,
though, against the opinions you've just heard.
But the way you put your question leads me back
to the far bigger question that I asked a while ago.
Why did you make the leap from Field Security
and volunteer to be parachuted into France
when the Nazis still had absolute control,
and Resistance was only a tiny flickering flame,
and the French still numb from defeat and deprivation,
and when the SD and Gestapo were hunting down[4]
resisters and the few foreign agents sent to help them
with brutal thoroughness, hunting them down like rats?
I never would have had the guts for that, no,
never in my wildest dreams.
— Well, I'll try to tell you. But I may need your help.

He puts out his hand towards his questioner, but lets it fall away
I think I would have been ashamed. In my deepest being
ashamed to stay . . . when others . . . Does that make sense?

Instead of responding, his double seems to be lost in memory
— Blowsy petals . . . a mild August evening on a terrace
outside a country-house in southern England. The scent
of roses mingling with the scent of death, the scent of battle.

I see a fair-haired captain, who'd been there and got back,
in the smart Highland trews of a regiment from Ontario,
not talking much and not a word about what
he'd seen as the tide was ebbing over the shingle at Dieppe.
And I feel a shudder, a deep inward shudder. Of duty?
Or the death-wish? Or of both? He has the air of wishing
he were still with his comrades who are dead or dying
or being marched off to German prison-camps. And I?
A subtle sense of shame is tangled with a deep resolve
to cast off what I'm doing (which I still believe in)
and share more fully in the stark discipline of the wars.

Shaking off these memories, he at last turns to reply
    Yes, that makes sense. In my own small way I felt
    it too, felt that, knowing what I knew about Hitler
    and the Nazis, I must offer myself up to necessity,
    to pitiless ἀηάγκη and its black wings and claws.

With the ghost of a smile, he picks up what his double has just said
    — So you see, your course was much the same as mine,
    and what I did not all that mysterious, and not
    in need of any very subtle explanation.
    — No! To die in the light was all that I was risking.
    What you risked was dying in the dark. That takes
    a lot more guts and a lot steelier resolution
    — I'm not sure I buy that. Or even see the difference.
    But if you want another layer of explanation,
    I'd say . . . I wanted to go behind the mirror.
    — To go behind the mirror? What does that mean?
    It's now my turn to say I can't buy that,
    haven't an inkling even of what you're saying.

A little exasperated with each other, they sink into silence: then the light changes, and the voice of the military historian comes again from the wings

While those two are cooling off, I'll try to sketch in for you the role of the Field Security sections that were attached to SOE, as Macalister's was. But it won't be easy. People in my profession tend to feel more comfortable when they have plenty of documents to depend on, like Churchill's correspondence with F.D.R., or the minutes of the Chiefs of Staff Committee, or a fistful of operation orders. We become a little skittish when the documents are few or fragmentary or non-existent. That was abundantly true of SOE, where some things of importance were never committed to paper at all, where such documents as were filed away were afterwards winnowed or destroyed, and where often all you have to go on is the evidence of survivors, who may have their own fish to fry or who may be still intimidated by the shadow cast by wartime security measures. I'll do the best I can, though.

But before I do you might like to know a little more about me. I don't play much part in this drama, and my master thinks that unlike the others I should always speak in prose. Still, I'm not a cipher either, I have a watching-brief, and some suppositions that colour everything I say. Unlike many of my colleagues, I'm prepared to allow a large part in human affairs to chance. History for me is the interweaving of chance and will and circumstance — and under circumstance I include long-term economic and social trends as well as such short-term items as the output of tanks and landing craft. Oh, one other warning. After a long immersion in the confusions and convulsions of our century and the ambiguities and deceptions of warfare, I may seem rather cynical, I'm afraid. But I still believe in one thing. About the only thing I care for now is courage.

Well, to return to the Field Security Sections assigned to SOE, their role was to protect the security of its Special Training Schools by keeping outsiders out and insiders in; or, less flippantly, by preventing the curious from finding out what was going on and preventing the trainees from giving the game away through careless talk in pubs and restaurants and so on. Sometimes that involved travelling with the same group of trainees from one school to another until their syllabus was complete — basic training, commando training, sabotage, parachuting, wireless training in some cases, and a final preparation for the field at Beaulieu Abbey. At other times a Field Security detail would be attached to a particular training school and might swan out widely from there to check on the security of agents who might be going through a final exercise. Sometimes they were in uniform, sometimes in civilian clothes. Often their work required a certain amount of more or less innocent deception. They might have to pose as just another trainee among agents undergoing training, or as a constable in the ordinary police force, or even as a member of the SD or Gestapo. So they gradually became inured to deception and also gradually took on more and more of the colouring of the Organization they served. So much so, that before long some of them wanted to be accepted as full members of the Organization and to be trained for service in the field. That was the case with John Macalister. He had been serving in the same Field Security detail as the irrepressible Harry Rée, they both applied together to be trained as agents to be parachuted into France, and finally they were both accepted. So it was by chance that the Field Security Section Macalister had been posted to was attached to SOE in the winter of 1941. But it was as the result of an act of will, of a deliberate decision, that he became a secret agent.

    Before I forget, though, there was another stage for both of them before they were on their way to France — a kind of half-way house. For a few months, they both became Conducting Officers for SOE. That meant that they became responsible for overseeing the final stages of the training of a few agents and for seeing them off from Tempsford Airport in Bedfordshire. But I don't imagine you want to learn more about these administrative minutiae. For the moment you've heard enough from me, I imagine, or more than enough.

As the light changes, his mother and his wife reappear. His mother speaks first
    — No wonder I was so bewildered!
    It was a caution. He would write one month
    from somewhere near the Channel coast
    and mention the Canadian troops he'd seen

and the next month he'd be in Invernesshire
commenting on how long the days were there.
But he never told us what he was doing.
A caution! I'd try to follow on the map
but it made me dizzy and dispirited.
Often I felt I'd lost my son already,
as though he'd fallen clean off the map
or had melted into Atlantic fog.

And then his wife
      — Lost to me, then!
                    After the armistice[5]
those years and years when I heard nothing.
Or if I heard it was less than nothing.
Three or four times I had a message
through a cousin living in Tunisia
and twice a postcard through Tangier.
But they were all so brief and cryptic
I almost wished that I had never had
them, they made him seem so far away,
so far away . . . Once I remember
praying for him in our Cathedral
and being surprised to realize that
my words all came from masses for the dead!
And then my cheeks were drenched in tears.

His mother resumes sorrowfully, quizzically
      — Was he already among the dead?
I asked myself when his letters stopped,
and all we had instead was a letter
from the War Office perhaps once a month
telling us only that "we continue
to receive excellent news of him."
"When the bough breaks" . . . was what
I murmured, "When the bough breaks . . ."

so that I hardly noticed the difference
when their monthly letters began to read,
"He was very well when last we heard."
That was all the news I could exchange
with the other mothers of soldier sons
when I'd meet them on the street in Guelph,
"He was very well when last we heard."
And I'd go on my way as calmly as I could.

His wife returns to those years in Normandy
In Lisieux, the emptiness of the streets
except for a few German staff-cars
and a few wheezy *gazogènes*[6] —
and the emptiness in my heart, in spite
of my deep love for my father and mother
who were my care through those hard years.
A dull daily monochrome of worry
as I queued for rations or for ration-books,
and everything tasteless, cheerless, mean;
the brackish taste of *ersatz* coffee;
the brackish taste of sorrow growing
everyday more soiled and shopworn.
Only at night would sometimes come
a presence in my dreams of love
miraculously returning to fill
my heart with sweetness, to fill me full
with a long absent sensual splendour.
But then the bleakness of awaking
and the bleakness of my weak pleas
to restore again my wandering love.
O quelle chimère, pauvre chimère,
And I would dress there by candlelight,
saying over and over childishly,
O quelle chimère, pauvre chimère!

As his wife and his mother glide away, he and his questioner reappear, seeming to have been brought closer by their mild confrontation and to be more at ease with each other. Now his questioner continues, but more indirectly

 — All of us have our own fantasies, our own chimeras,
fantasies of sexual prowess or sexual felicity,
or fantasies of power, or fame, or wealth -- a gold-mine
gushing a constant stream of dollars in our lap
or a beautiful girl picking us out from a thousand others.
I've sometimes wondered if it was some secret fantasy
that led you to risk your neck the way you did.
 — What kind of fantasy do you think it was would beckon me?
 — I don't know. A fantasy like that is often deeply private.
 — But you must have had some kind of fantasy in mind.
 — Well, perhaps the glamour of dropping from the skies,
accomplishing your mission, and returning to applause
and to having a row of ribbons pinned on your chest.
 — Often the bravest men wear only the ribbons of death.
You must know that. That's something every soldier knows.
But if you want to know, I *did* have fantasies
although not the kind of fantasies you're thinking of.
I was a radio operator, remember, and they're tied to their sets
and their fixed schedules, however often they need
to move from house to house. The fantasy I had,
the dark chimera I had to live with while I was training,
was that German detector vans would zero in on me
while I was sending. Then the door opens and I am looking
down the business end of a German Luger or a Belgian Browning
and I am caught with my earphones on, and the set before me.
That image would always make me wake up sweating.
 — I see I must have been mistaken. I'm sorry.
But somehow I'd got the impression that among the agents
sent to France were quite a few who were fleeing
a scatty life or one that they'd made a mess of;
and that others were seduced by some imagined glamour
in the moonlit sky, by some strange magic in the weave

of parachute silk that might float them into
a glossier world than any they'd ever known before.
But that impression may be quite mistaken, too.
— We were a mixed lot, that's for sure. Some of us
well brought up and well to do. Some of us middle-class
like me. Others with hardly a pot to piss in —
if you'll forgive my slipping into soldier's language.
— A gunner's ears are hardly so sensitive as that!
— Well, there we were, aristocrats and dead-beats,
businessmen, artists, solicitors, successes, failures,
bound only by impatience to get on with it
and thirsting to be doing something useful on our own.
But don't imagine that many of us — perhaps half a dozen —
were lured by dreams of glamour, dreams of glory.
You may not know that two of our greatest stars
had been grammar-school masters before the War,
and good ones too, who were conscientious objectors
until they decided that *this* war must be fought.
I knew both of them, Harry Rée and Francis Cammaerts,
and afterwards — in Buchenwald — learned what they'd done.
It was Harry who masterminded the sabotage operations
at the Peugeot factory that made gun-carriers for the Wehrmacht,
and tank tracks. It was Francis who was liaison officer
for that ghastly business in the Vercors that drew off
two German divisions that might well have made a difference
in the cauldron boiling around Falaise that summer.
— You don't know, you couldn't know, what they both
did afterwards. They both went back to teach in grammar-schools.
— I didn't know, but I'm not surprised. They both were solid,
solid. I wish someone could have said the same for me!
— Perhaps they did . . .
                    And perhaps I should be ashamed
to be asking you about your fantasies when I'm not prepared
to tell you mine, to let you see the glimmer of gold foil
flickering down the brain's dark twitching labyrinths,

alleys much darker possibly in my case than in yours.
— There's no need to apologize.
                                        It's not so strange
to want to know the reasons for what might seem a desperate choice.
And I've admitted that perhaps I didn't know myself.
But what I've not admitted (*Now he is lost in his own thoughts.*)
is that I was conscious of something avid, something ravenous,
deep within me. Avid for what, though? Ravenous for what?
         (Islands of greenness, of blessedness,
                  blest islands that float beyond
                           the green limits of my childhood city
                  islands beyond the limits of Guelph and goodness
                     islands of peace and order, but with passion
                              and mild vehemence ordering them
         blest islands of passionate intent
                     lawful but never to be entirely caught
                              within the green toils of government.)
Never truly knowing what I was ravenous for,
yet often thinking that I'd been reared for some great test
       for some great task.
That was a dream still cradling me from my mother's nurturing.
But then she thought that true of every mother's son
— incredible! — thought that was true of everyone,
thought all of us were sent here on some special errand.
How difficult a gospel to believe in, and impossible
ever to put in practice or ever to fully act upon!
Still . . . still . . . a tincture in my heart
that would never leave me utterly, in those pulsing chambers
a trace of rainbow that bound me still to common clay
and would never let me soar too long above myself
but would always bring me back to earth
would bring me back to fellowship with our dying clay.

So, some great test . . . and wondering if I could meet it,
wondering if I had the nerves for what might lie ahead

in a land that had lost its bearings and was full of guile.
Always I had been able to come up with what it took
when the moment came. But what if the moment was obscure,
the questions baffling, and my answers all foreseen?
What if the fear was worse, the torments worse, the torture?

Five

After the effort of struggling with his own thoughts, his own conflicts, his amiability has faded. Now he turns to face his questioner with a kind of controlled impatience

— You asked for reasons. There are reasons the heart has, you know.
— I know that. I don't want to pry. But I wonder if you
were misled about the risks.
                                                 — I don't think so.
Like everyone else who volunteered to be dropped into France
I was interviewed by the Organization before being accepted.
(It comes flowing back to me . . .) My interview was at 4 o'clock
one afternoon in an old hotel just off Trafalgar Square
that had been requisitioned by the War Office. To avoid being late
I arrived a full hour early and killed time in the reading-room
of Canada House looking at old copies of the "Guelph Mercury."
Then, as I left, I had a word with the soldier at the door,
who was a lance-jack in the tartan of the Toronto Scottish,
and that somehow made me feel that I was saying good-bye
to Canada one last time.
                                         — Like Canadian troops
sailing out of Halifax Harbour past Point Pleasant Park?
— Yes, a little like that, I suppose.
                                       The room was large and empty.
Only a trestle-table covered by a grey army blanket
with two folding chairs, one for me in my sergeant's uniform,
the other for a middle-aged Captain (on the General List, I think),
who asked me first to tell him about myself. And I did.

And then asked me why I wanted to volunteer. And I told him.
But since he had my file in front of him, I think he skipped
some parts of his routine. Some parts he didn't skip, though.
He gave his usual warnings (that I'd heard about already),
first, that I'd have only a fifty-fifty chance, if that,
of getting back alive, and, second, that if I was caught
I would almost certainly be tortured — little did he know!
But he didn't underestimate the risks. In fact,
he recommended that I think it over before signing on
and emphasized that I could always withdraw "with honour"
if ever I should change my mind. I told him there and then
I didn't need more time to think it over, since I'd
been thinking about it now for weeks. And I knew within myself
that I could never withdraw — with honour or without it —
after my shaming indecision in the summer of 1940.
No, my decision now was like the image of a drawn sword,
that lay on the table there between us, glittering.

There is a rustle of voices overhead or from the wings as his wife comments, and then his mother, and then an agent safely returned, his mission accomplished. His wife speaks first, alternating with his mother, and finally the successful agent offers an interim judgement

    — He was too brave.
                      — He never fully knew himself.
    — He should have waited.
                      — He was far too highly strung.
    — But the courage!
                      — And without a core of courage
how can anything ever be achieved, can anything be built?
And courage shadowed by weakness may be the most precious
of all, since it carries sweetness into the heart of the building,
carries it like honey into the hollows of the honey-comb.

As though not having heard these other voices, his questioner and he now pick up the threads of their interrupted conversation

— You say you told the interviewer why . . . ?
— Yes. And he understood. And if *you* want to understand
you'll have to coax your imagination to guess what it was like
being attached to the Organization without being in it,
simply serving perhaps as a despatch-rider taking messages
from one training-school to another, or up to London,
or checking on the security in pubs and dance-halls of agents
under training, or masquerading as one of them in the courses
they were taking, but leaving them before their final leap,
and enduring often the contempt of those who went
for those who stayed.
                      And in the process inevitably
learning more and more about the subtle secret threads
that laced Britain to the Continent, learning
about the dropping zones for parachutists, and the landing
fields for the small Lysanders that came and went
with each full moon.
                      And inevitably learning more
and more about the coded signals that came from secret
senders in supposedly safe houses, until — what happened?
a raid? a shoot-out? a betrayal? — silence, blackout,
and then the long arduous task of building a new wireless link.

Gradually from these and other sources — from aerial
reconnaissance, from air-crew shot down and then passed from hand
to hand until they trudged across the Pyrenees, and no doubt
from other sources far too secret for me to know about —
a picture was constructed, a kind of mirror, a huge radar-screen,
of what was happening inside France. Not only where
von Rundstedt had his headquarters, and his subordinate commanders,
but also much more homely details: how rationing
was working, who was going hungry and who was eating well,
what passes were needed to circumvent the curfew,
which were the most dangerous check-points on the Paris *métro*,
until the fascination of the puzzle grew so great

for some of our people in the Organization, I was told,
that conditions in Paris and the provinces became
more real than anything in Whitehall or a Bayswater flat.
— And was that true of you? Were you under the same spell?
— No, it was a different spell for me *(dreamily now)*. Europe for me
was always mysterious, always "the mysterious Continent."
  (Who was it said that was true of woman? . . . Freud, I think . . .
     "the mysterious Continent")
Its otherness was complete, a woman outstretched and violated,
in my dreams a woman dark and dishevelled, ravished,
a creature of blood and darkness. And then I'm dreaming of my wife
(whom I've hardly heard from since our daughter was delivered, dead)
dreaming of her as shut up in a dark tower in Normandy
until a lover from afar should come to waken her.
One night I stayed gazing across the Channel, hour after hour,
over the barbed wire and the tank-traps on the beach,
not thinking of intelligence reports about a France
criss-crossed by flickering courage, and apathy, and treachery,
but simply sighing my soul towards the mystery there —
until at last I had to make my way back to Beaulieu Abbey.

A kind of Scotch mist hangs over most of the time
I spent in the training schools, either on attachment
or as a conducting officer or as an agent under training.
But some things stand out. The chief lesson I carried away
from the lectures and demonstrations on unarmed combat
was, "Always try to kick your opponent in the testicles."
(Yes, and I remember the instructor's relish in telling us that,
and repeating it over and over so that we wouldn't forget.
It was the relish that was to come back to haunt me, later,
much later, and in rather different circumstances.)
Then Scotland itself. The Western Highlands facing Skye,
where there really *is* Scotch mist that chills and drenches
you as you're crawling on your belly in a fieldcraft

exercise or fumbling with explosive charges to blow up
a mock-up bridge or scrambling through an assault course.
But sometimes as the mist and rain are moving off
there can be glorious moments of sheer indigo cliffs of cloud
towering over dark hills of hunter green. It was then
that I most often felt a stirring of the blood, a kinship
with my people who left those glens such years ago
and through Canadian generations passed on to me
my slim inheritance of Highland pride and stubbornness,
even some traces of a passionate Highland hothead.

Among my friends I'll mention only one. And that one
Harry Rée. For six months as a Field Security detail
we played cops and robbers with wireless operators
strung out on their last clandestine exercise before
being sent to France. At night we'd masquerade
as the SD or Gestapo and break in on their safe-houses
to test how well they knew their cover stories and how well
they'd managed to conceal their sets and outspread aerials.
By day we'd act as couriers, meeting them in public parks
or lavatories, and putting them through their paces once again.
It was always lively being with Harry. He made life more vivid
than anyone else I ever knew. And we'd talk endlessly.
About philosophy. Or law. Or education. Even intelligence!
We both agreed intelligence was a world of mirrors —
many of them cracked. (Harry had decided views on everything.
And as you've probably guessed by now, part of my story
is that I was often given as partners men far more
decisive and self-confident than I was, Harry Rée
for one, or Francis Cammaerts, or Frank Pickersgill,
all of whom either by nature or by hard experience
self-confident to a fault.) It was Harry who decided
that our French was just as good as many of the agents'
whose security we were testing, so we should volunteer.

Now the story is interrupted by a confusion of voices from the wings, among which can be distinguished his wife's voice, his mother's, the voice of several other agents, and of a woman who was a high staff officer in Baker Street

"His French was good enough while he was with us in Normandy. But I can't believe that, after being so long in England, it was adequate for the mission he was sent on. I often wonder why he was ever allowed to go."

"It takes a lifetime to learn a language properly. My son had only a few short years, and most of that time had to be spent on other things. He should never have been sent, never."

"Why on earth were Pickersgill and Macalister sent on such a dangerous mission? I often asked myself in Buchenwald, where I got to know them. Their French was so faulty they could never hope to pass themselves off as Frenchmen."

"In 1943 there were many foreign workers in France, and Macalister's cover story was good enough to let him pass as one of them. The judgement of the only agent who ever escaped from Buchenwald can't be overlooked. But his opinion needn't be taken as the last word on everything."

"I agree with Francis Cammaerts. Remember that Pickersgill and Macalister both wanted to go. And try to remember the pressure we were under in Baker Street. The need was great. And there were so few who were willing and qualified to go. It was a risk we had to take."

After the hubbub caused by this dispute has quieted down, they go on, unflurried by anything that has been said during the clamour around them

— So we agreed to volunteer and go behind the mirror.
Is that something that you see more clearly now?
— It's clearer, yes. But what's clearer still is, as I've said,
that I never would have had the guts to volunteer
for what you did, and be parachuted into the lion's den.
— I don't imagine what you volunteered for was a picnic either.

I've been dreaming back to try to show you how it was for me.
Don't you ever find yourself dreaming back to that time too?
— Yes . . . there are few days I don't taste something of the colour
of those weeks at Cassino and along the road to Rome in May
of '44. But all my decisions were commonplace compared
with yours. That cut to the quick of our wicked, wounded time.
— Who is there can say what's commonplace and what's not?
It was thousands, and hundreds of thousands, of commonplaces
that made the difference, even to the outcome of the Resistance.
— By your decision you risked dying in unfathomable dark.
Like thousands of others, I only risked dying in the light.
The odds were shorter, the risks much easier to prepare for
— *(Self-deprecatingly)* To die in the dark, to die in the light, isn't
    it the same?
And perhaps, who knows? I was risking more than I possessed
Had I enough in my wallet to cover the stake I'd made?
— That's close to what I'm trying to say. The stake you'd made
was almost infinitely greater than anything I'd put at risk,
or any of thousands, hundreds of thousands, of others like me.
— I failed. But many of our people were true heroes and successes.
And that goes doubly for the French resisters, who had their families
to consider. Without the Normandy landings, though, what would
it all have come to? Without the brave, ordinary resolution
of guys from Louisville, and Liverpool, and Saskatoon?

But don't let's argue. You spoke of the colour of those weeks
in May of '44. Tell me about that. I'd like to know.

As he hesitantly accepts the invitation, it's as though he were being reabsorbed into the Italian light

                            The colour of those weeks?
                   Sand-coloured, dust-coloured, khaki-coloured
                             with patches of red
                 (no, not of blood, though there was that, plenty of it —
               the red-patched sleeves of the 1st Canadian Division)[7]

        the khaki-coloured dust-storms kicked up by jeeps and guns and trucks and tanks
            thickening the atmosphere, parching the throat,
        until it thins out at the level of so many castled hills,
      opens out (even higher) into an immense blue cloudless sky.
And through that lucid atmosphere the silky ripple of outgoing shells
— they would sound differently to the enemy —
                            and the thunder of incoming shells
hurtling like express-trains towards you, scaring you shitless.
And the combatants running, crouching, digging, digging for dear life,
the *contadini* cowering in cellars, or at intervals being shepherded
safely through the lines, but still with a long low lament of
        "*Rotta, tutta rotta.*"
And now my ear-drums catch more of the excursions and alarms
that cut through the dusty, far-off, viscous atmosphere:
"Recce in half an hour!" or (louder) "Recce in ten minutes!"
or (loudest of all) "Mike target, mike target, mike target!"[8]
that puts everyone on the *qui vive* at the command post and the guns.

Two weeks of firing thousands of rounds of smoke shells
and high explosive, and staring up at Monastery Hill and Monte Cairo,
then moving off down Highway 6, the rifle companies leading
(with the engineers), and then our field guns, moving almost
every day and plotting new targets and barrages every day,
through a haze of battle shimmering like a fiery furnace.

As though continuing the almost trance-like recall of those weeks by his double,
he quietly interrupts
       — The heat-haze after a long hot summer day in Guelph,
that's what your haze of battle is uncannily leading me back to.
Husbands and fathers out in their shirt-sleeves watering the lawn,
their children minnowing back and forth beneath the hose.
Our next-door neighbour, Mrs. Burrows, out on her porch,
crocheting, and noiselessly rocking in her rocking-chair.
And I've been out riding on my bike down to the river
where families have come with their picnic-baskets, hoping to catch

a few wisps of coolness from the water, and where a sandlot
baseball game is now winding down. It's dusk as I'm returning.
Before putting my bike away, I take one last look at our park,
where there's still a film of heat-haze round the roof-tops and the trees.
Mrs. Burrows puts down her crocheting, but still is quietly rocking.

From the wings come shouted fire-orders, louder this time, fortissimo even —
"MIKE TARGET, MIKE TARGET, MIKE TARGET! FIVE ROUNDS GUNFIRE! FIRE!"
— It is the former artilleryman who is the first to react
    — That rips the glaze off reverie.
    — And what is shown underneath?
    — I don't think it's anything on the road to Rome.
What I see outspread before me is something below Coriano
and not far south of Rimini. That's where we lost
three gun-crews in a morning. Black pillars of smoke
rising from the gun-pits. In the narrow coastal plain
between the Adriatic and the Apennines . . . And fear. The sweat
and stench of fear. I don't think I was ever more afraid,
except perhaps one night near Pontecorvo, when the whole battery
was in convoy on a sunken road, nose to tail, with the enemy
dropping chandelier flares and strafing us with his Messerschmidts.
    — *(With almost a lawyer's satisfaction at scoring a point)*
So what you risked that night was dying in the dark,
no different from me.
                    — But it *was* different, far different.
Perhaps I should apologize for my tropes and figures.
For me, dying in the light is, yes, dying in the light,
but also dying within an order that's still holding, if only just,
and in ways that can to some degree be prepared for.
You look as though you doubted that? Perhaps prepared for
by taking your life out from behind your ribs and setting it to
one side, by giving it up before going into action,
like taking a wrist-watch off and setting it on a table.
And there are simpler ways, ways still less metaphysical.
I remember somewhere on our way north to the Gothic Line[9]

watching one night a gunner sew by candlelight
new red patches on his tunic-sleeves. And who shall say
what those patches meant to him? The regiment? Or Canada?
Or some larger cause? At least it showed and sealed his loyalty
to something greater than himself which he was ready,
if need be, to die for. But that was to prepare for dying
within an order that still held, within a skein, however
tenuous, that stopped well short of the hiss and lapse of chaos.
But for dying in the dark? . . . to prepare for that?

The light changes, and they half-turn aside from each other into their own soliloquies, his double speaking first
    — On a meat-hook! on a meat-hook! To prepare for that?
    — The schools taught skills, or thought they did, to combat fear,
had ways of trying to prepare us for interrogation, torture.
But the lessons never fully took with me, perhaps
they never fully took with anyone, perhaps there lasted
deep within the hardening frame of bone and muscle
some cells' silent sob of inward fear and dissidence.
So it was with me. With decision and acceptance came
euphoria. But not for all that long. Then back seeped
              doubt to enter
        like frost in masonry
doubt whether I was staking more than I possessed
doubt whether I was banking on a fearlessness I might not have
            doubt entering
        like frost in masonry
      day after day, deeper and deeper
    and the daily effort to combat it.
That led to tenseness, and sometimes to a drying up
of natural instinct that I had trusted in to see me through.
And the effort to hide how tense I was made me still more tense.
I wondered, Was it visible! Were others sure to see it?
One day with Francis Commearts at a restaurant in Soho
I thought that he was on the brink of mentioning it,

he spoke so feelingly of my transferring "to the field."
The moment passed. I felt relieved. Yet in a way regretful,
since it left me to fight this psychomachia on my own,
aided only by exhilaration jetting up from youth and strength.

Now, as they turn towards each other again, he goes on speaking about preparing for what lay ahead, but more casually
— Of course I was apprehensive, often, about that dark
unknown. But I had been apprehensive about parachute training
at the school at Ringway airfield, afraid that I'd be too scared
to jump, or that the parachute wouldn't open, or that I'd break
some bones on landing. That fear had burned off quickly, though,
into the near bliss of floating on air along the slipstream,
and then a gentle tug as the parachute opens, and then
a moment of brief celestial quiet, and then my body
rippling freely to cushion the crash of upcoming earth.
So fear soon vanished into something much more like addiction.
— You make it all sound easy. Did you really think
it would be that easy, your dropping into occupied France?
— I didn't know. I never minimized the risks.
But I knew that the fears I felt, that anyone would feel,
could be controlled. So I wasn't nervous when Frank Pickersgill
and I were given our final orders at Orchard Court
and then our final briefing in a shed at Tempsford airfield.
We would be flying by dead-reckoning to Chenonceaux[10]
and after picking up the Château in the moonlight
an ordinary Michelin map would lead us to the dropping-zone.

Six

> *O Chenonceaux*
> *quelle âme est sans défauts*

That was the little jingle I was saying to myself
as the Halifax trundled out along the tarmac, turned,
and then lumbered heavily aloft, higher and higher,
to avoid the flak there might be over the French coast.
I tried to concentrate on my cover story, on the life and times
of Jean-Charles Maulnier, and then on my operation orders,
going over them point by point. But I kept coming back
to Chenonceaux, imagining it as chalk-white in the moonlight,
turreted and towered, with pale glimmering arches astride the river,
its gardens full of roses and of orange-trees in tubs,
where there had been great unhappiness, as everywhere,
but also times of great *douceur de vie*, as I imagined them,
and where such times might come again if all went well.

> *O saisons, O châteaux*
> *quelle âme est sans défauts*[11]

Then the pressure on my ears as we're descending.
The red light flashing as we approach the target zone.
The despatcher unbolts the hatch and hooks our parachutes to
    the static line.
Red turns to green. And I sling my legs out into space.
Then "Go!" — and down I drop. With Frank right after me.

Once on the ground, the mood turns more to questioning.
Those dark, dense woods? Are they protective or malign?
Dark shadows moving through the trees? Are they friends or foes?
I've turned my ankle, but apart from that all's well,
and members of the *réseau Adolphe*, or *sub-réseau*, rather,[12]
are gathering in the canisters that floated down behind us
and folding up, and hiding, the yards of parachute silk,
and loading the canisters (packed with arms and ammunition)
on to a two-wheeled farmer's cart that looks a little
like a tumbril. And, because of my ankle, I'm ensconced there,
amid the hidden weaponry, as we follow back roads through
low-lying level flatlands and the smell of new-mown hay
to a bridge across the river that points the way to our safe-house.

Once there, as first light tries to shine, we glimpse a region
of woods and marshes, a country sprinkled with ponds and pools,
brambly, a country that seems made for poaching — or resisting.
But I've gone on now long enough. Now its your turn,
since you sometimes seem to know more about me than I do myself.
— I do know some things. But I'm never sure whether they're true
or not. I'll try, though, on condition that you interrupt
whenever I'm mistaken. By all accounts you stayed
a few days in the summer-place of a family of resisters
while your ankle healed and Frank's documents were improved,
keeping under cover during the day (since the Luftwaffe
had the area under close surveillance), whiling away the time
in talk beneath the oak trees, talk about sabotage and
subversion, yes, but also about Sartre and Aragon and Saint
Augustine, and the relevance of Plato's allegory of the cave.
— (*Drily*) At that point it must have been Frank who was doing the talking.
Philosophers usually have a low opinion of lawyers and the law.
— From now on the story becomes uncertain. Some say you left for Paris
on the Sunday, some on the Monday. Some say the weather was still
unclouded June, others that it had broken — and so on.

— Well, back to me, then. And the film of that year's longest day.
    (It's a film that I've often had occasion to wind, rewind,
        to replay endlessly.)
It was on the Monday that we left for Paris. The weather was
moyen, as the French say, neither one thing or the other,
grey, cloudy, overcast, *couvert*. The *sub-reseau's* chief,
Pierre, was driving, with Jacqueline, his deputy, beside him
(as though man and wife) and Frank and me behind them.
I tried to convince myself that everything was normal,
that this was a normal trip to Beaugency to catch
the train for Paris. And there were moments when I succeeded.
How wild this is for France! I'm thinking, How thickly wooded!
with a dense underbrush of young saplings, brambles, bracken,
beneath the oaks and evergreens — and here and there
tall stacks of cordwood, much as you might see them along
the roads in parts of Canada.
                        But then my mind swerves
inward. To our secret orders: to our rendezvous with PROSPER,
the leader of the widespread network fanning out from Paris,
to the sub-circuit that Frank is to organize round Sedan
in north-east France — with me as its wireless operator. To my
security checks, both true and false, for use as I am sending.
To my cyanide pill. To the reasons I might have for crunching it.

Then back to the road. Unreeling evenly . . . up to a road-block
manned by field-grey soldiers with some *feldgendarmerie*.[13]
My heart is in my mouth, but Pierre smooth-talks us past
that checkpoint (which shouldn't have been there at all) on to the next,
only a half-mile further, where Frank and I are ordered out
and marched between two guards towards the nearest village.
As we approach it, Dhuizon trembles with the specious unreal clarity
        of a *trompe-l'oeil*:

                              a
                             slim
                         black *flèche*
                      atop a village church
                  that centres a small village square
          surrounded by chestnut-trees and a bright momentary collage
                         of village shop-signs
                  CHARCUTERIE. ALIMENTATION. BOUCHERIE.
                         AUBERGE DU GRAND DAUPHIN.
But now the *trompe-l'oeil* is tumbling down into a melée
of German soldiers in the square we're being marched through
around the Church and towards the Mairie.
           (Did I pray as we passed by? I can't remember. I don't think so.
                    . . . perhaps, though, I was being prayed for.)
In the Mairie we're taken for questioning to a large panelled
oblong room that might have been the mayor's office, or
council-chamber, or both. But now the mayor's desk has been
pushed back and a German sergeant is sitting at a trestle-table,
and round the walls are ten or twelve resisters (or so
I guessed) scooped up by the same operation, the same *rafle*.
I thought I answered the sergeant's questions well enough.
But something made him suspicious, he ordered them to search me,
and soon my money-belt was on the table there between us.
Before long Pierre was brought back, bleeding from a wounded leg
and roughed up badly. And with him the package that had been
disguised so cunningly, containing our transmitters-and-receivers,
a fresh supply of wireless crystals, and messages *en clair*
from Baker Street to PROSPER and others in the PROSPER network.[14]
Once everything had been discovered, a Gestapo officer
handed the rifled package back to Pierre, and said
with icy irony, "I think that will be sufficient, sir."

Was it my accent that gave the game away? Or some nervousness
of mine in answering? Or something said by the resisters caught
before us? Those questions I had to live with in the months to come.

Then we were handcuffed and taken out to be driven to Blois.
The last thing I remember as we were man-handled into
a German staff-car was a small clutch of old men and boys
(either too old for service, or too young) who came out from the bar
across the way from the Mairie and waved a little as we left.

The light changes. He and his double are faded out, and a stream of comments comes from the wings:
First from one of those who watched from the door of the Bar de la Mairie
— We saw them marched into the Mairie under escort and then, a few hours later, come out in handcuffs. It was only afterwards that we heard someone say they were Canadians — and came from the sky. Now they have entered into legend in our region.

Then his wife
— I see it even more clearly now. He never should have been sent.
His French was not nearly good enough.

Then his mother
— As I knew from the beginning, he was far too highly strung. No,
he never should have been sent.

Finally the military historian
— It would have made very little difference whether his accent was good, bad, or indifferent, whether he stumbled over his replies or not. The PROSPER network had been penetrated by the Germans months before, and the Gestapo were only waiting for what they judged was the right moment to strike.

The light darkens as he resumes
Driving to Blois . . . driving deeper and deeper into the forest.

At a turn of the road what was that I heard them say?
That they were driving us to Gestapo Headquarters there?

        Towering darkly over the river was the way I pictured it,
        a Château whose stairways ran runneled with blood and crime.[15]

        To the dark tower
                  to the dark tower
        fee, fi, foh, fum
                  the dark tower.

Now the light changes to focus on his mother and his wife, who are both praying for him, but in their different ways:
His mother's prayer
        Mary Immaculate, Mother and Virgin,
        Mother of God, and Mother of this Church,
        you know the suffering of a mother for
        her suffering son as he goes to trial,
        you know the frailty of all flesh,
        frailty that lives on even in the strongest,
        intercede now for me with your dear Son
        that my son's tissues, his tenderest tissues
        be not torn, violated, destroyed,
        guard over what is most vulnerable in him,
        his eyes, his sex, his tender neck,
        protect him in the lion's den
        with all the mercy of a mother's love.

His wife's prayer
        Mary, I beseech you for my husband
        as he draws near his hour of torment.
        I know the strength that has glorified me
        and filled me, filled me with new life.
        But I have known too his diffidence,
        his self-distrust (for all his strength),
        the inconstancy in his net of nerves,
        such flickering — as there is in all men —
        of confidence and strength, but more

in him than most. Summon his courage
for the trial. Brandish the sword of Michael
before his eyes and make him strong,
make him all hero in this darkest hour.

He continues as before, leaving it uncertain whether or not he has heard what his wife and his mother have just said
fee, fi, foh, fum
                        to the dark tower.
But it wasn't to the towering Château we were being taken.
Only to a squat ordinary house behind the railway station.

His double comes forward solicitously
— What was it happened? What was it like. Tell me.
— How could I tell you? You would never understand.
— Perhaps not. But try. Even if it's only a few words.
— One word will do.
— And what's that?
— Grim.
— That's all?

He walks angrily away. Then in the empty silence, from off-stage comes a high-pitched scream. And another. And another. When he returns, he has difficulty for a few moments in controlling the muscles of his face and in keeping his hands from twitching. . . . As soon as he begins to speak, it is clear that he is speaking mostly to himself
— Belts, belt-buckles, truncheons, army boots,
all the ordinary paraphernalia of ordinary torture.
But how to express the inexpressible? or how to prepare for it?
I had been forewarned, so they claimed, of what to expect.
The experience was different. Pools of darkness. Pools of evil.
The eyes of the interrogators, the eyes of their henchmen, brimming
with evil. Obviously human, as they consulted their dossiers,
yet obviously wicked, as they made me cry out with kicks

to the testicles, and took relish in it, relish in cruelty.
What of my defences as the black water swirls higher?
Already they seem to know everything I've been taught to protect.
My name, where I came from, where I'm supposed to be going,
even arcane details about Baker Street, it's personnel, its procedures —
to say nothing of the PROSPER network, and its sub-circuits.
My eyes cloud over. But not only my eyes. My mind
before long is reeling with vertigo. The time comes when
I hardly know what I've told them and what I've refused.
That was part of the torture.

His double quietly intervenes
— The official summary in the Foreign Office reports
that both of you, both you and Frank Pickersgill, "stood firm."
— What does that mean? To say that we both "stood firm?"
— That in your interrogations you "gave nothing away to the enemy."
I am quoting the exact words of another official report.
— I suppose I should be grateful. But how could anyone tell?
— After the War, your interrogators were themselves interrogated.
And that was the unwavering testimony of them all.

He begins to put out his hand to his double, but then lets it fall away, as though still troubled and doubtful
— Perhaps they had their own hides to think of. Perhaps
they wanted to ingratiate themselves with the victors.
Perhaps that was what they thought they wanted to hear.
— There is other evidence, subtle, yet in a way more conclusive.
The officer who conducted the post-War interrogations
for SOE told me that when an agent has given something
away, you expect soon afterwards to get some reflection of it.
There was nothing like that after you both were arrested.

Now, as they are facing each other, he puts out his hand again but this time doesn't let it fall away but takes the other's hand. The stillness lasts for a few moments while their hands are clasped. Finally it is broken by his asking half-humorously

— Since you know so much, perhaps you could tell me how and when the PROSPER network came to be compromised?

The military historian, from the wings

That is my cue for trying to set out what we know and what we don't know about the penetration of the PROSPER network. We know that it had been deeply penetrated well before Macalister and Pickersgill were dropped into France on the night of the 15th of June 1943. In particular we know that the network had been compromised by the activities of Henri Déricourt, a French airlines pilot who had been recruited to serve as the Air Movements Officer of the French section of SOE, with special responsibility for arranging landings and pick-ups for the light Lysander aircraft that were now running a ferry service between France and Britain, to supplement the parachute drops. That Déricourt was working for the Gestapo or SD — by now they were almost indistinguishable — in Paris as well as for SOE in London, has long been known for certain. He was keeping his German masters informed about SOE operations in France and was arranging for them to make copies of the messages being sent by Lysander from Baker Street to its agents in the field.

But beyond that all is "night and fog" — to use a sinister German expression. Here are some of the unresolved questions:

Was Déricourt not only a double, but a triple, agent, as has been plausibly argued? Was he working, not only for the Gestapo on one side of the Channel and for SOE on the other, but also for the British Secret Service, for SIS in Broadway Buildings off Parliament Square, against SOE in Baker Street? The evidence is unclear. So how can we tell?

Had he been planted on SOE by someone in SIS, as has also been plausibly argued? I wish I knew.

A few in the British intelligence community knew that the PROSPER network had been penetrated by the enemy. How far down had that knowledge filtered by June of 1943? That's still a mystery.

Were Pickersgill and Macalister dropped as unwitting actors in a broad scheme of strategic deception, in the expectation that if they — and probably PROSPER too — were picked up by the Gestapo, such information as they might let drop would help to encourage the belief that the Second Front was to be opened in 1943 rather than in 1944? We know that there was such a broad scheme of strategic deception. But as to its scope and whether it reached down to F section of SOE . . . who can say?

Was Churchill himself involved in such deception? That may seem far-fetched. But some people have said so who ought to know. And war ministers don't often leave much documentation behind about meetings with their secret agents, or about their personal participation in schemes of strategic deception. So how can we tell?

And with that we have traversed another landscape of mirror and mirage, another region of broken mirrors.

This time he has been listening intently, and now offers a terse comment
 — Well, I suppose I must be content with that.
I'm glad anyway to be cleared of passing information
to the enemy. To be scooped up so soon was bad enough.
 — Some evidence goes rather further than that and suggests
that you both faced questioning in a mood close to defiance.
A witness who was present at the interrogations at Blois
testified at a post-War trial that neither of you would say more
than that you were officers who had been parachuted into France,
and that one of you added, "I know what is in store for us.
I have only one request: that my family in Canada
be notified of the circumstances of my arrest and execution."
 — That must have been Frank. He was an authentic hero,
much more demonstrative and aggressive than I ever was,
or ever could be. In the early months of the Occupation
while he was interned in Brittany, one night in the cell
next to him he saw a French soldier clubbed to death

by two German guards. That tempered his courage to a white
heat of fury that stayed with him right to the end.
In the 'thirties he had been slower than you, slower even than me,
to grasp what the Nazis were up to. Step by step, though, he had come
to the conviction, like the rest of us, that Hitler must be defeated.
After that night, conviction was kept fuelled by blazing anger
so that he always seemed to be capable of almost any feat
of fearlessness, with an almost unquenchable will to resist.
After we'd been brought back to Paris from prison in Poland
he nearly escaped one day by breaking the neck of a wine-bottle
and using it to slit the throat of one of the SS on guard.
I never could have done that, never. I've confessed I had inklings
at times of having been raised for some great test —
but not for slitting another man's throat with a wine-bottle.
There was always a difference. My mood hardened as time went on.
But I never could have done that, never. Frank had learned
what I was never able to learn, how to confront the world like a hero.
Of course there were times when I hated his guts. You can't be manacled
to another man for hours, even days, on end, without coming close
to hate, or to love, or to both. And there were times when I hovered
between almost-hate and almost-love. Well, that hardly matters.
To the end he had greatness of mind and greatness of heart.

Seven

From the distance comes a faint breeze of ragged trumpets, that gradually swells into a full but short-lived fanfare. Now it's the double's (and poet's) turn to speak

Strip *gloire* and *grandeur* from their place in the pediment.
But heart's blood is still needed as much as ever before.

Topple the ridiculous Sun King from the height of his pedestal.
But what is a *cour d'honneur* without heart to defend it?

It's the heart's blood of courage, with its systole and diastole,
that runs through and supports everything mankind has made.

The minuet, the flowering cadenza, are nourished by heart's blood.
The artist, as much as the athlete, depends upon heart.

What of the other manifold virtues? They would be as nothing
without the circlings of courage sent to sustain them.

It takes many forms, this primal animal virtue,
But a soldier's honour may stand as a blazon for them all,

whose calling demands of him courage, endurance, loyalty,
and the ultimate commitment to be ready to stand and die.

So the far-off fanfare may fade but is never uncalled-for.
Even peace-keepers still need to be clad in the soldiers' virtues.

The fanfare is sounded again. But this time loud and clear. As it fades, now they slip back into friendly conversation, unembarrassed by trumpets
— After a few days in Blois you were driven to Paris?
— Yes, to Gestapo headquarters on the Avenue Foch.
— That would be No. 84, then. I remember it well.
— How could you possibly know that? I can't believe it!
— It was the Canadian Embassy after the war. I was there often . . .

(Lapsing into a mood of perhaps too indulgent reminiscence)
The broad sweep of it, that is what stays with me most. The broad
sweep of the roadway from the Etoile out to the Bois
and a broad *allée* alongside it, gravelled and sanded and swept,
then green lawns with oaks and plane-trees and chestnuts, to a narrower road
running in front of tall stone facades, six or seven storeys high,
with fenced private gardens to shield the rooms on the *rez-de-chaussée*.
— All I ever saw was the black water in the gutters.
That was all that told me I was in Paris, what ran in the gutters.
— I'm sorry. For a moment my own memories swept me away.
I was in Paris for weeks, even months, at a time
for the Reparations Conference and the Paris Peace Conference
and would often be in and out of the Embassy. And I remember
I never went into the washrooms without a deep visceral shudder
because of what I'd been told the Gestapo had done there.
— Let's skip that. There'll be plenty of that before we're through.
— But isn't it true that suspects were repeatedly plunged
into ice cold water there and repeatedly brought close
to drowning in a brutal attempt to make them talk?
Isn't it true . . . ?
— Let's skip that.
(On another tack, deliberately) I was even more bewildered there
than I'd been at Blois. It was like an icy sleet-storm
that I seemed to be moving through for hours at a time,
wondering what they knew and what they didn't know.
At Blois their questions were mostly about arms dumps and circuits.
In Paris they were more interested in codes and cyphers.

Why, though? Already they seemed to know everything,
and that made me, might have made anyone, feel lost and adrift.
Worse still was the sense that I might be caught in a vast web
stretching from Paris not only to the Oberkommando in Berlin
but also perhaps to our own command in Baker Street.
That chilled to the bone. In the end I came to believe
that what they wanted of me was not so much information
as to break me, before handing me over to "night and fog,"
to break me, as they'd broken hundreds of thousands before me.
With that came a few rays of light and warmth. What I had
to do became simpler, to refuse to do anything shameful.
They wanted me to send their fake messages on my set to London.
That I would never do, that I would die rather than do.
Do I make it sound almost rational, the way I reacted?
Then don't be deceived.
All the time I was riddled with fear and pain and loathing.
— Isn't it true, then . . . ?
—   Yes . . .
"I know nothing. I know nothing."
Nothing!
Only water flooding and freezing my lungs,
through the cold rippling water
faces leering, jeering
rippling into mocking masks of wolves, foxes, grizzlies.

Now I'm lying naked on my back on the cold marble floor
looking up at the white and gold of the cornice
I was dead and am alive.
In a few minutes I'll be dying again.
I don't know whether I want to die or to live.

At last I'm returned, we're returned, to the prison at Fresnes.
I don't know why, but a submerged taste for living returns,
making its way through the taste of blood in my mouth,
a wry bitter coppery taste that lasts a long time.

Slowly a taste for living returns. But how to live?
Painfully, thickly, I begin to think — or try to think —
to think about that. Even begin to think as the door clangs shut
and I am alone.

With a gradual change of light, his double melts into the shadows, and the main stage is left bare, except for Macalister. At the back of the stage, though, a German sentry begins to walk back and forth, and continues on sentry-go until almost the end of the story

    To think about how to live there, in solitary confinement,
never knowing from one day to the next if it would be your last,
if the tread of the sentry would stop at your door and hustle you out
to execution or to another long session at the Avenue Foch;
how to live in a cell some ten feet deep by five feet wide
        (I soon paced it out);
how to put in the twenty-four hours on a ration of *ersatz* coffee
for breakfast and at mid-day half a mess-tin of weak soup
with perhaps some cabbage-leaves thrown in, or a few slices of turnip,
and, shortly after that or shortly before, the day's ration of bread,
just enough to keep body and soul together — and after that nothing.
So most of the day, every day, my guts were writhing with hunger.

As anyone would, I tried to fill in the time with whatever
I could dream up, with pacing up and down, or reeling off aimless lists,
or remembering my earlier life with my friends, my family, my wife.
But before long I found those contrasts too risky. They could soon
drive me mad if I let them. Sadly I had to kiss them good-bye, good-bye.
So what was left? Often nothing. And that could drive me mad too,
the impingement of nothingness on nerves stretched tight as piano wire.
What to do? I am lying in bed wrapped in my thin ragged blankets,
aching all over and hungry as hell. What to do? What to do?
That afternoon I had heard gulls screaming between two blocks of the prison
        (not the cry of returning spring
            but the cry of predators eager for their prey)

Now those birds of prey seem to be attacking my vitals,
their claws in my eyes, their beaks picking my vitals to shreds.
What to do? My animal pride had been stripped away. Could I make
something, though, out of all those years I had spent mostly in thought?
For that I would need a problem or problems to gnaw away at
as a beaver gnaws away at a stand of young alders or poplars.
At first my intellectual pride, what was left of it, tempted me
(because of where I was and the slipperiness of the jeopardy I was in)
to try my teeth on the issues that might seem most important,
"Why are we here?" "Can our life be given a meaning?"
But I soon backed away. I had come to doubt not only
my own aptitude for questions like that but even to doubt whether
the human mind is so fashioned as to be able to answer them.
So, some questions that were not so large but still formidable . . .
Before falling asleep I was murmuring, "Why war? what does it come from?"
then, "What is it in society that can produce such a rank growth as Hitler?"
I would choose one or the other — or both of them — to spar with,
to wrestle with, to have as my companions in "solitary."

A few moments of total darkness. Then as the light half-heartedly returns, his double returns with it, and comments
    — It's been hard enough to follow you to the Avenue Foch and to Fresnes.
But to add those nettles and brambles to interrogation and torture . . . !
    — You would have done the same, or else something similar.
If you wanted to stay sane, you would have been forced to.
    — It seems a long way from the quiet of Oxford, broken only by bells,
or from the cloister that's a basin for cascading bells at Toronto.
    — Fresnes could be quiet, too, when there was only the tread
of guards and sentries, or orders relayed from one catwalk to another.
    — And no books! nothing to turn to if you came to an impasse.
I could have found that enough to stop me dead in my tracks.
    — *(Drily)* Each morning a corporal came round with an issue of toilet-paper
and it was mostly pages torn from old books long discarded.
    — Not exactly fodder for disinterested speculation, I imagine.

Not exactly a match for the holdings at All Souls or the Bodleian.
— (*Deeply serious again*) At first I turned to the great theorists, hoping for
   their help
To work out how a proud civilized nation could give itself over to vileness.
What would Weber have said? Or Vico? But they weren't replying.
Perhaps I had forgotten too much of what they had written.
Or perhaps they hadn't encountered what I had encountered.
At any rate that hope soon faded away. I was on my own
with a more than formidable antagonist in a long dark tunnel
that stretched all the way from Fresnes to Rawicz and beyond,
only a little less dark than the Bunker at Buchenwald,
that tunnel of nightmare length with steel cells on either side
for every kind of imaginable or unimaginable brutality —
to try to explain that, not only by the events of the decade
that led to it, but by diving into the murk of the black water
that spawned it.
   — (*Cautiously*) Do you mind my interrupting?
You've spoken of Rawicz. And I've seen other references to it.
But I know nothing about it. And no one else seems to.
— No wonder. At Rawicz we were nothing. But we'll soon come to that.

After brushing the question aside, he goes on, but more tentatively
   The great theorists weren't coming to my aid.
   So I began with what couldn't be doubted.
   With vileness, . . . *that* I had felt in my own flesh,
   that I had seen in the eyes of my torturers.
   But not only there. In the stench and venom of a whole regime . . .
   that came snaking down from Himmler and Hitler.

   It was easy to get that far. But to get beyond that?
   I couldn't just let myself wallow in a brew of self-pity and hatred.
   How to move on from there?

   I stared at the *graffiti* on the walls of my cell, often it seemed
   for hours at a time, sometimes waiting for the clank and clatter

of the food trolley, but sometimes waiting to find a way forward.

When an opening finally came, it was faintly ridiculous.

> It was an image of one of our instructors
> at one of the SOE training-schools,
> a former policeman who was expert
> in close combat (or silent killing),
> in using the commando knife he had perfected,
> and in the most lethal kinds of karate chops.
> What is it I hear him repeating?
> "Kick him in the testicles, kick him in the balls"
> repeating that over and over and over.
> And me entering that in my memory,
> as though in a notebook, but always with
> some scruple of reserve, as though
> I doubted whether I was cut out for it.
> Odd that in my reflections at Fresnes
> that echo should resonate so loudly,
> should take on the resonance of a leading case.

— (*His double as though anxious to show that he has been following*)
Are you saying — as so many did — that if we were to defeat
them we would have to become more and more like them?
— Well, yes, I suppose. But I really meant something much larger
than that. The resonance I experienced came from the knowledge
that in all of us there are veins of malice, cruelty, venom.
It was the relish that the instructor took in the black arts
he was teaching us that convinced me of that, convicted me of it.
Of course, ordinarily, those impulses can co-exist more or less peaceably
with other more benign impulses of generosity, kindness, affection.
Even in Germany that remained true, even after all the vile
draughts of foulness and filthiness that the Nazis brought with them.
— That doesn't surprise me. It comes easily to me to say I agree.

One afternoon in the pursuit to Rome
our jeep had to swerve to avoid running over
a dead German paratrooper lying in the road.
I looked at his staring eyes and tarnished
insignia and could not help thinking,
"How ludicrous it would be to believe
that every German soldier is guilty
of all the crimes of the regime it is
his lot to serve! That would be monstrous."

— One afternoon in the prison at Fresnes
the cell-door opened and a corporal came in
very shyly, sheepishly, timidly,
and out of one of his tunic pockets
took a pair of glasses I had dropped
on the way back from another long
session with my friends at the Avenue Foch.
He was so frightened and vanished so quickly
that I didn't even have a chance to thank him.
But the glasses stayed with me to the end.

— In Italy I was always scared stiff of losing my glasses.
Without them I would have been helpless, utterly helpless.
But I don't want to slip back into my own pale recollections.
I want to hear what conclusions you came to about how
a civilized society can relapse and produce a Himmler or Hitler.
— Well, I'll tell you, if you don't mind hearing them set out
like articles in a code or a statute. Please forgive that
and please don't forget where I was as I beavered away at them.

Eight

With a change of lighting, the stage becomes brighter. At the back, the German sentry is still pacing to and fro. Then, from off-stage, this alien atmosphere is pierced and modified by the low voice of a seeming interloper calling in the tones of a court crier, "Oyez! Oyez! Oyez!" Then . . .

In every society there are brutes.

In everyone there are impulses of the brute. Call it original sin.
Call it part of our animal nature. It's there.

In a reasonably decent, well-tempered society the brutes are never allowed to come to the top. They are kept in their place by a hierarchy of different psychological types, ranging from the most brutal, the most violent, to the most intellectual, the most religious, the most imaginative, the most sane. However often it is threatened, in a good society that hierarchy is never overcome, it still retains its integrity.

In a reasonably well-tempered personality the impulses of the brute are also kept under control and are seldom, if ever, allowed to come to the top. Here, as in society, there is — or should be — a hierarchy.

But the hierarchy of types in society and the hierarchy of impulses in individuals are both fragile. They can both be disturbed, subverted, overthrown — with catastrophic results.

> If the metabolism of a reasonably functioning society is too deeply disturbed by either internal or external events, the result may be as catastrophic as the coming to power of the Nazis.
>
> If the metabolism of an individual is disturbed by either internal or external trauma, the results may be equally catastrophic.
>
> The two systems are linked. If a social system becomes deranged, the results will soon be transmitted to all but the strongest of its members.
>
> Equally, if enough individuals lose their balance and their sense of the necessary subordination of other instincts to those that should be sovereign, the results will soon be transmitted to the whole society.
>
> The aim, then, not only of statecraft, but of everyone must be to avoid the occurrence of either of those two calamities.

Well, those were my theses. I was tired by the time I had come
to the end of them. By then we had left Fresnes and travelled to Rawicz.
Sometimes I was content with them. At other times I felt
I had been trying to comprehend the incomprehensible.
Best perhaps to think of them not as articles in a code
but as sketchy preliminary pleadings. But was I acting for
the prosecution or the defence? I'll leave that for you to decide.
— You know I'm not learned in the law. Far from it.
But that sounds to me more like some outsider summing up,
some jurisconsult called in to act as a friend of the court.

You say that by now you and Frank were at Rawicz in Poland.
I thought I knew a good deal about concentration camps,
but I'd never heard of Rawicz.
                                — I'm not surprised.
It wasn't a concentration camp, but a great gaunt

fortress-like prison, built in the nineteenth century
(like Fresnes) when that part of Poland belonged to Germany.
— Why do you think the Gestapo sent you there? It seems strange.
— I haven't a clue. Only a few guesses, that may not be worth much.
It may have been a snafu, a mistake. Even the Gestapo made them.
Or it may have been a compromise between those in the Gestapo
who wanted to despatch us at once and those who wanted
to keep us on ice — and nearby. Or it may have been merely
because they could be sure that there we couldn't escape.
It was a long way away, Rawicz. A long way from Paris.[16]
A long way from London. A long long way from Toronto. Or Guelph.

There was a touch of frost the night we arrived
that made me think of the tang of October in Canada
(it was less colourful, though, without any maples).
We had been on our way a long time, in filthy box-cars
mostly, to reach at the end of the journey a prison not all
that different from Fresnes, the food a little better perhaps,
the sanitation a good deal worse, no running water,
a leaky bucket to wash in, another leaky bucket in place
of a toilet, the guards perhaps a little more arbitrary
than they had been at Fresnes, a little more ready to shoot
a prisoner for "disobeying an order," or for no reason at all.
     (that perhaps reflecting the difference in Nazi theology
         between the proper place in the world
            for the French and the Poles)
At first I thought I had seen it all before,
the two prisons seemed so much the same. But I was wrong.
Stalking through the corridors came not only brutality but madness.
A louche spectre. With a fell feline odour. A drifting contagion . . .
brewed it might be from the pride and hope and despair
of a country torn every which way over the centuries
and now held in the brutal vise of *two* occupations.

A few nights after we arrived a boy with bulging eyes

screamed, and jumped to his death down an open stairwell.
And that same week an older man ran berserk
on all fours, animal-like, down a prison corridor
until he was clumsily shot dead by a frightened guard.
All this was happening in a tongue impenetrable to us,
and that sheathing made it seem worse, or at least more bizarre.
— I'm thinking of Yiddish or Hebrew? But I may be mistaken.
— There were no Jews at Rawicz. Hitler's agenda for them was more final.
But his agenda for the Poles was terrible enough — their nation
to disappear, their élites to be destroyed, the rest to be serfs.

As Christmas approached, preparations for it went forward.
But even there hysteria seemed to play a part — maybe
because of the rumours circulating about the course of the War,
which sometimes were true but as often as not wildly untrue,
so that hopes and fears were paired in a dizzying tarantella,
in a fever of excitement that ran through the prison like typhus.

As for me?
I'm alone, as I am mostly,
trying to finish my work-quota for the day,[17]
when I hear a clear deep voice from along the corridor,
repeating, as before a prayer-wheel,
"Fucked up and far from home"
innocent enough as a soldier's expression
but so reverberating in my brain-pan
that I think it may crack my skull.
It will drive me mad, mad!

He comes forward a few paces and is staring straight ahead, his face a grotesque mask, as he shouts
    FUCKED UP AND FAR FROM HOME!
and then once again
    FUCKED UP AND FAR FROM HOME!

As the echoes die away, there is a long pause until he begins to come to himself
>I am trembling after that burst of hysteria. How to find
>a way back to sanity? a way back to my normal self?
>Perhaps I might breathe more calmly by thinking of some
>others who would die far from home — in sands of the desert
>(where tanks of the Afrika Korps or the Eighth Army had laagered)
>or in the Arctic off Murmansk, or in Pacific islands
>with names still shadowy then to us in Europe, names
>that were only names or hardly even that, but where
>day after day men were dying in swamp-ridden jungles.

Now his mother and his wife reappear for a few moments towards the back of the stage, but on opposite sides. His mother speaks first, distraught
>Where is he now?
>Was that his voice
>that I heard last night
>or only the end-of-October wind
>that whips down everlastingly
>the last of the leaves?

And then his wife
>Where is he now?
>Last night in my dreams
>his soft brown eyes were piercing me,
>his sad brown eyes.
>"When last we heard" now seems
>such a sad time ago.

Without seeming to have heard them, he continues in an answering vein
>— That night as I fell asleep I was back in Guelph
>>(comforting as they might be at first
>>>such dreams had a treacherous edge
>>>>on waking the effect could be lethal)
>
>I am walking down our street, past the Park, past Mrs. Burrows',
>towards the Hundred Steps . . . if that name means anything to you?

  — Yes, I know them. They come at the far end of Metcalfe Street
and lead down over the railway tracks to the part of town
that spreads out at the foot of Nob Hill.
              — There's a watery moon,
and I'm standing at the top of the Hundred Steps, looking out,
as faces on the other side of the tracks begin to materialize
in a drift of silvery fog, faces of school-friends I've known,
faces of people I've seen on the street but not really known,
others whom I've perhaps one day interviewed for the "Mercury,"
but all of them imprinted with a story of their own.
A composite of faces, whirling like a whirl of leaves.
And that now spreading, spreading, to involve thousands,
hundreds of thousands, millions
    (even in sleep
       I am half-conscious
           of being frightened
              by what I am watching)
all the millions lost in the War, faceless yet singular,
what they cherished, what they loved, their solitariness,
their secret anxieties, what made them what they were,
that swirling and rising, in a vortex, in a great whirlwind,
into a sky that is torn and ragged, indifferent . . .

the winds of the world, the winds of War, that swept them away.

The long silence is at last broken by his double asking
  — Did you have the chance, either at Fresnes or at Rawicz, of tackling
that other question of Why war? Where does it come from?
  — Aren't you expecting a little too much, a lot too much, of me?
What if I toss the question back and ask *you*, Why war?
Where does it come from? It's a question you must often have pondered.
  — I don't think I can answer. I'm getting out of my depth.
  — You can't desert now. It was you who started this, you know.
  — But where should I begin? It's such a difficult question.

— Begin wherever you like. I'm leaving that up to you.
— Then I'll begin with fury, the fury at the heart of the sun,
the molten fire and fury that swirls at the core of the earth,
the fury of desire (never gentleness alone) that produces a child,
the heat that lives on furiously in a young man's thighs,
the swirling fury that erupts in Krakatoas and Santorinis
(and in geologic time Krakatoas are a dime a dozen),
the fury of burning hydrogen — with all that primal fury
around, is it any wonder that we still have wars?
That's hardly the question.
                              — To deny the validity of the
    question,
is one of the oldest ploys there is. I'd thought better of you.
— *(Shaken by this unexpected onslaught, his double is beginning to stammer)* I'd rather raise the question of how to tame and harness
that fury. With reason. With reason set like a jewel
in the claws of animality. With reason, irradiated
by sympathy, by sympathy and imagination . . . *(giving up)*.
— I don't disagree. But what you're suggesting may be harder
than you think. As you would know if you'd travelled with us
en route from Paris to Buchenwald in August of '44.[18]

In March the Gestapo had us flown back from Rawicz to Paris
in an attempt to have us help them — what a hope! —
in the radio game they were then playing against Baker Street,
and we were grilled again by their thugs in the Avenue Foch,
the rue de Saussaies, the Place des Etats-Unis (it was there
that Frank killed one of the guards and almost escaped.)
But by August, as the Allied troops approached closer and closer,
they had had enough of that and had us shipped out to Buchenwald
in one of the last trains to leave Paris before it was liberated.
That journey I remember as about our worst trial of all.
— I've often wanted to ask when it was worst for you,
ever since I learned that, in those few days of freedom you spent

in a hideout in the valley of the Loire, you talked under the oak trees
about sabotage and subversion but also about the relevance now
of Plato's allegory of the cave.
— Please don't get us wrong.
None of us thought we were philosopher-kings or had had
a vision of the Idea of the Good. But in so far as we
had had some inkling of it, we thought we were under an
obligation to go back into the cave, back into the dark.
I doubt, though, if any of us imagined just how dark it would be.
— But what made it so especially dark, that last journey to the east?
— (*Again speaking mostly as if to himself*) All the way handcuffed
in two or threes, and for part of the way manacled
round the ankles as well. The compartment we were in,
all nineteen of us, so small that only one couple
or two at the most could lie down at any one time —
and that made for arguments and recriminations, natural
enough, inevitable perhaps, but disconcerting among
friends and comrades all sworn and united in the same *équipe*.
Just under the surface smouldered and simmered a fractiousness
that once in a while would erupt in outright antagonism
and, but for the handcuffs, would have led on to fist-fights.
Then, it was August, and the August sun burned down on the roof
of the compartment, making it hell, and a hell with no food
and only a few sips of water. My throat was a furnace.
— And I gather you'd been badly beaten up just before leaving?
— Yes, that was the Gestapo's going-away present for us.
I was ashamed of my body by now, two teeth knocked out,
my arms bruised black and blue, shit caked on my legs.
I used to be proud of my body, my prick always hard
when I wanted it to be, and often when I didn't want it to be,
my build a strong athlete's build that was sturdy enough
for the rugby field or for long nights of pleasure or study.
To say good-bye to all that was harder than you might imagine.
I tried not to grieve over most things. I grieved over that.

There wasn't much time for grieving, though. Late
on the second day our train was spotted by RAF
fighter bombers, who took us for a German troop-transport,
I suppose, bombing the engine and swanning back and forth
along the rest of the train, spraying machine-gun fire.
We still were handcuffed, remember, and locked in that hellish
compartment, wondering if we would all be incinerated
there — and by our own planes . . . That would have been too much.
(I hand it over to the connoisseurs of chaos and to other
aestheticians of violence.)
        — And how was it from then on?
— We were transferred . . . No, that's enough!
Some things have faded and some things I've managed to block out.
And that's one of them, the rest of our week-long journey eastward.
But this may give you a faint glimmer of what it was like:
It was a relief for us all to be delivered at Buchenwald.

Nine

The stage is now swept by searchlights that give off an eerie bluish-green light. While they are sweeping back and forth, the loudspeakers also begin to give tongue, first blaring out:

  Achtung, achtung, all prisoners are to report to the Appelplatz
and then:
  Achtung, achtung, the following prisoners are to report immediately to the Tower.

A few minutes later, the loudspeakers fall silent, the searchlights are turned off, and the lighting returns to what it had been before, except that now there are some glints of winter in it, as there often are in late August in many parts of Canada. Macalister turns to question his double

> — I'm assuming you know a good deal about Buchenwald already?
> — I hardly know how to answer. But I didn't need all that hubbub to remind me of the watch-towers with their searchlights and machine-guns.
> And the two fences round the camp of electrified barbed-wire.
> And the Appelplatz, where roll-calls often went on for hours, roll-calls of the living and the dying, of the dead and nearly dead, where the dead had to be brought in on the shoulders of the living to make up the tally for each day's deadly arithmetic.
> And the Bunker, with its rows of punishment cells, where prisoners were beaten to death, injected with phenol, or killed by some other means that happened to be that week's whim of the resident monster.

— Yes, all that's right on target. But there's one thing missing.
The stench. The filthiness day after day. Dysentery rampant.
Overcrowded tiers of bunks. I leave that for you to imagine.

But that's hardly fair. Because it was unimaginable.
And our lot was far from being the worst. There were circles
far lower than ours. That's one reason I can't be an adequate witness.
Some things I can witness to, though, that you haven't mentioned.

A miasma

a moral miasma hanging over the camp

like the smell of burning

of burning flesh

that curled up

from the square squat chimney

not far from us.

Even at Rawicz or Fresnes,
even in the most gruesome of prisons there remain some traces,
however faint, of justice, of judges, of trials, of sentencing,
of the possibility of appeal, of pardon, of release.
(Some higher court might some day issue a writ of *certiorari*.)
There was nothing of that at Buchenwald. There it was all
arbitrary. You might survive. Or your throat might be torn out
by one of the dogs the SS kept to act as their surrogates.
It was all a lottery — and a lottery always loaded against you.

We were there so few weeks, Frank and I, that we scarcely had time
to find our feet in that moral quagmire. But we could see,
anyone could see, that part of the horror came from prisoners
(prisoners much the same as ourselves) being licensed to do the work
of their masters, often with authority over life and death.
That suited the convenience of the SS apparatus:
it economized on manpower. But it also had a deeper
and more diabolic purpose — to break down human
solidarity, to break down all human ties and loyalties
except those to the Nazi party and the Third Reich,

to reduce the individual prisoner to the struggle for survival,
to break his spirit as well as his body, to annihilate him.

Have I said — I think I have — that we were privileged?
all of us who came on that so demonic transport from Paris?
We weren't issued the usual striped prisoner's uniform
but were clothed instead in ridiculous hand-me-downs.
We weren't sent out to work. We were enumerated not in
the Appelplatz but in our own Block in the quarantine zone.

>   We were privileged, yes,
>   but to what end?
>   Did it bode
>   well or ill?

Some thought we would soon be transferred to Oflags (I didn't)
and treated as regular prisoners of war. Some thought (I didn't)
we were being held for exchange with an equivalent number
of enemy captives. Some thought we were being saved (I didn't)
to be used as bargaining chips with the soon-to-be victorious Allies.
Don't think I was more prescient or stoical than the rest.
My moods would vary, like everyone else's. But I had hardened.
I had given up hope, but was fighting to hold back despair. . . .
Then, the optimism that I couldn't share was fed by plentiful rumours.
But I imagine you had plenty of rumours in Italy, too?

His double is quick to reply, as though knowing what is fast approaching and trying to stave it off as long as possible
    — Yes, we were awash with rumours that autumn in Italy.
With the Gothic Line broken, Kesselring would withdraw his crack troops
north of the Po. Anyway, the war would be over by Christmas.
The Germans were so short of firewood they were cutting down
the *pineta* near Ravenna. As for the 1st Canadian Division,
it would soon be transferred to France, or England, or Yugoslavia.
    — Our rumours also told us the war would be over by Christmas.

Even before that, the Allied armies would reach Buchenwald
and free us in a matter of weeks. Or we would be rescued by paratroopers.
Or in another scenario, pinpoint bombing would destroy the SS barracks
and open the gates, and breach the barbed wire, for us to escape.

I didn't contradict the optimists. I didn't argue. I didn't disagree
with the rumour-mongers. But I never believed in rescue or escape.
At times I allowed myself to credit the rumours, but never for long.
At times I went along, or seemed to go along, with plans for escape,
especially when they seemed to be floated only to keep up morale.
I didn't even argue with Frank, when he would talk aloud
with himself about a post-war career in Canada, wondering
whether it should be in the Foreign Service or in university teaching
or the National Film Board. I didn't argue. But I was ruffled,
since it was all I could do to hold my guts together for the end.

His double, looking away, far away, as he speaks in an aside
— Yes, I know, I know . . .
Once in Italy I saw a guy who'd been hit in the belly
trying to walk a few paces as he held his guts in his hand.
— I said very little. But I didn't believe in rescue or escape.
I had hardened. I knew myself better now. My only resolve
was to die as well as I could when the time came.

As the light changes, he and his double are faded out, while his mother and his wife reappear, standing not far apart towards the middle of the stage. It is his mother who is first to speak

        What was it that came to me on the wind?
        I can only think of one word, "Waste."
        He might have been a Justice or Chief
        Justice. But I think less of his lost future
        than of his darling presence, his smile,
        his own affectionate way of speaking,
        his love for his father and for me.
        All that destroyed and gone to waste!

Then his wife
>If you had known France enslaved,
>had known how much he valued freedom,
>how much he hated the Nazis' programme
>for subject peoples and the Jews,
>how much he feared their lawlessness
>would spread world-wide, your words
>would alter. Yes, "waste." But if the waste
>of war is still the price of freedom . . . ?

His mother again
>Now I stop at every Station of
>the Cross, praying for hope against hope.
>There where a chapel in the apse
>shows Mary cradling Her wounded Son,[19]
>I kneel and, gazing up at Her,
>ask Her forgiveness for so often
>likening my own dear son to Hers.
>But, Oh, the heartache and the waste!

Then his wife again
>I too pray at every Station of
>the Cross, pray for him from my soul.
>But think, Who was it taught him
>that everyone is precious in God's sight?
>And that belief cries out against oppression,
>cries out against the wicked folly
>that sets one race above all others,
>licensing every kind of cruelty.

His mother again
>I know that everything you say is true.
>But how could I foretell that truths
>I taught him would carry him so far

       away, and into so deep a dark?
       You try to teach me how to see
       more clearly, to see him as a hero.
       I know, I know, I need your schooling.
       But still to me he is my only child.

His wife again
       Over the years and over the waves
       let our tears be joined, giving no comfort
       to those who passing by, speak lightly
       of any transcendent sacrifice.
       I share your pain, I share your loss.
       Let our tears be joined in grief and pride
       that one so dear should have been so brave,
       standing so steadfast to the end.

At last they embrace — briefly and lightly — and then melt away into the shadows. As they disappear, from the distance again comes a muted fanfare, to which his double, as poet, again begins to add words, varying them a little as he goes along
       Strip *gloire* and *grandeur* from their place in the pediment.
       But heart's blood is still needed as much as ever before.

       Topple the ridiculous Sun King from the height of his pedestal.
       But what is a *cour d'honneur* without heart to defend it?

       It's the heart's blood of courage, with its systole and diastole,
       that runs through and supports everything mankind has made.

       It takes many forms, this oldest and still cardinal virtue,
       from the inborn courage of natural heroes like Heracles,

       with nerves and muscles so perfectly mingled and meshed
       that for them the most extraordinary feats seem nothing at all;

       to the commoner courage of those who have had to overcome
       fear, learning how with bravery to outface the world;

to a rarer kind, of those who never could learn
that lesson, but struggled with recalcitrant nerves to the end.

All deserve tribute and win their place in the Pantheon.
But there may be particular virtue in those whose heart-beats

have stayed caught in a noose of implacable nerves,
since that courage has ties to the condition of us all.

Now the fanfare is sounded again, loud and clear, but this time with the sob of wood-winds being gradually added to the blaze of trumpets.
After it dies away, their conversation continues, the prisoner in Buchenwald commenting with only the slightest hint of irony
— We were privileged, as I think you'll remember —
privileged too, after a few days, to wander about the camp
and savour the sights. We took in the Appelplatz,
and the Tower (and gate-house) with the Bunker on one side of it
and the offices of the SS on the other, and Block 46,
where it was rumoured they were using prisoners as guinea-pigs.
We had leisure to sort out the different nationalities —
the Soviet prisoners-of-war, the Poles, the French —
and to become familiar with the various insignia,
green triangles for the criminals, red triangles for the politicals,
yellow triangles shaped into a Star of David for the Jews.

It was the Jews who were in the lowest circle of all.
To the SS the Slavs were a despised inferior race.
But the Jews were on a far worse level than that —
hated the most, despised the most, abused the most,
given the least to eat, beaten, tortured the most,
and so suffering the most, succumbing, dying the most.
When I saw the bodies of Jews stacked like cordwood
outside the crematorium, I felt ashamed to be a man,
it made me feel ashamed for the whole of our species.

It was a Jew who one day was a member of the latrine Kommando
and happened to slip into the raw open pit of the cess-pool.
And an SS guard then stepped on his clutching fingers
until he finally drowned in a deep pool of shit.

Did I see that? Was I told about it? How did I know it?
I'm not sure. I had blocked out some things and others were blurred.
But I believe it. I know it was true.
Most of the time at Buchenwald I was in a dream-like fugue,
a dream-like flight from myself and from where I was,
of a kind often found in epileptics and psychotics.
But I was never more sane. It was only my dreams,
my dreams whether asleep or awake, and twilight dreams
between sleep and waking, that kept me almost whole — and sane.
And now I drift back to them . . .

Ten

The light changes as he is dreaming back, first to the colour of lucid flame, then to a nebulous whiteness, and then to a torrent of blacks and reds

      A fiery furnace
     a sheer transparency of flame
    a few young men walking through it
      bright-coloured doublets
      all unscorched unscathed
     until with a smell of burning
    fire starts to singe their bright hair
          All the time I was waiting
       A radiance
     a background radiance
    as though left over after creation
   a voice a face diffused to brightness
   the voice the face of mother? wife?
    a radiance moving ever outward
      a far vanishing point
           I was waiting
     A taste of ice and fury
    the taste of pomegranate seeds
      a grenade exploding
     the hiss of seeds spat out
     an intimate explosion
       of ice and fury
  bringing down floods of blood and chaos
           I was waiting

Emerging sometimes from those dreams to look on horror,
and once at least to look back on lost felicity.
Around the corner of a Block near ours in the quarantine zone
glimpsing green rolling farmland rippling away towards Weimar[20]
And that night remembering . . .
>   green fields round Guelph
>   ripening to harvest
>   with sea-green corn
>   silky and tasselled
>   billowing
>   uplifting like a ship
>   our Church of Mary the Immaculate
Then the next afternoon . . .

Now the loudspeakers blare out:

Achtung, achtung, the following prisoners from Block 17 are to report at once to the Tower: Benoist, Hubble Kane, . . . Macalister . . . Pickersgill

Achtung, achtung, the following prisoners . . . Macalister . . . Pickersgill

Achtung, achtung . . . Macalister . . . to the Tower

— *(After the long silence, his double now finds his voice, to ask in a whisper)* You knew then?
— I knew then. I only hoped it would be short.

The historian takes this as his cue to intervene again
>   But it wasn't short. We know how Macalister died. And Pickersgill. And
>   the twelve others who were executed with them that day in
>   September. There were four other agents who knew them all at
>   Buchenwald, and who survived, miraculously. And they heard from the
>   Special Kommandos, prisoners who were forced to serve the ovens in
>   the crematorium until, after a few weeks of service, they were

themselves killed and cremated and their places taken by another batch of Special Kommandos. That's how we know. And what we know is that, on orders issuing from Hitler himself, they were executed in the same way as the conspirators against his life on the 20th of July. Slowly, that is, so as to prolong their death agony as long as possible. Hitler had a film made on the spot of how Field Marshal von Witzleben and seven other of the conspirators were killed, and he watched it with relish time after time, showing it to select groups of friends and to groups of the SS. The film hasn't survived but watch the screen and you'll see what it showed.[21]

> The conspirators are brought in, one after another, stripped to the waist, to a large cell in Plötzenzee Prison in Berlin. Steel meat-hooks are hanging from an iron rail fixed to the ceiling. One after another the prisoners have wire noosed round their necks, which is then looped around the meat-hooks. They are then lifted up and dropped, but gently so as not to break their necks. Their trousers are now ripped off. Now they are completely naked, their feet dangling off the ground, their arms and legs twisting in grotesque contortions. Death comes after twenty or thirty minutes of slow strangulation. Hitler laughs and laughs.

It is left to his double, and poet, to finish the story

    And he was hanged the same way.

    Don't close your eyes. Don't turn away. I'll help you.

    Being beaten up by the SS. His face swollen, his eyes almost shut.

    Then a coil of piano wire noosed round his neck

    and that looped round a meat-hook cemented into the wall.

    Then being hoisted up and being dropped softly, softly,

so that his neck wouldn't mercifully be broken.

Then turnings, twistings, twitchings, twitterings.

And then the iron maw of the ovens.

(After a pause, impersonally, almost hieratically)

So what is left? I ask of the dawn wind

as morning rises blue and bruised, like a boxer.

What is left? I ask of the silence at the heart of the whirlwind,

ask of high heaven, with its ragged indifferent clouds.

Ash, ash in the wind, in my mouth, in my nostrils.

Ash, with the ribbons of death streaming around it.

A proud sad archangel turning in the wind.

A song, a song strangling in sobs.

Notes

[1] University College, the old central College of the University of Toronto, was built between 1856 and 1859. Architecturally, it is an eclectic mixture of Romanesque and what might be called Ruskinian Gothic. Macalister was a student there between 1933 and 1937, being enrolled in the Department of Law, where every year he headed his class, taking First Class Honours in every subject and graduating with a Rhodes Scholarship.

[2] At Oxford, Macalister took a First Class in Jurisprudence in 1939, and the following year took a First Class in the B.C.L. examinations. That same spring he was also awarded the Certificate of Honour for standing first among all the candidates in the Bar Final Examinations in London.

[3] The order in which Macalister attended SOE's various Special Training Schools is perhaps immaterial and, at any rate, is now impossible to sort out, since he attended some of them as a sergeant in the Field Security Police, others as a conducting officer for SOE, and still others as a full-fledged agent in training.

[4] The SD was the security section of the SS, which had Heinrich Himmler as its chief. Originally the Gestapo had been the secret political police of the state of Prussia. But shortly after Hitler came to power in 1933, it was taken over by Himmler in his capacity as Hitler's Minister of the Interior. Thereafter it became increasingly Nazified, and the distinction between it and the SD became increasingly blurred. That is the justification for the widespread custom of referring to both services indiscriminately as "the Gestapo."

⁵ On the 22nd of June 1940, an armistice was signed at Compiègne between France, then governed by Marshal Pétain, and Nazi Germany.

⁶ *Gazogènes* were automobiles powered by large floppy bags of producer gas instead of gasoline, which was unavailable during the Occupation to almost everyone in France except members of the Wehrmacht.

⁷ At the final battle for Cassino, which began on the 11th of May 1944, the 1st Canadian Field Regiment supported initially the 4th British Division. Later, at the breaking of the Hitler Line and in the pursuit to Rome, it rejoined its own division, the 1st Canadian Division, whose units could all be readily identified by their red shoulder-patches.

⁸ "Mike target, mike target, mike target" is the ritual formula for the call from regimental headquarters for all the guns in the regiment to fire on a single target.

⁹ The Gothic Line was the name for the German defensive position running roughly from Pisa to Rimini. The battles to break through it in the fall of 1944 were some of the bloodiest and most costly of the whole Italian campaign for the Allies.

¹⁰ The Château of Chenonceaux includes a long gallery spanning the River Cher, which is a tributary of the Loire. The Château is only a few kilometres from the area where Pickersgill and Macalister were dropped early on the morning of the 16th of June 1943.

¹¹ Some indication of Macalister's interest in French literature is provided by the inventory of his (pitifully few) belongings which was sent to his widow in the spring of 1946 by his executor in Oxford. Most of the books cited individually are in French and deal either with French literature or French history.

¹² The *réseau Adolphe* was a sub-circuit of the much larger *Prosper* network in northern France. It was led by Pierre Culioli, whose field

name was *Adolphe*. His courier and principal lieutenant was Yvonne Rudellat, who had been trained in Britain as a SOE agent and in the field took the name of *Jacqueline*.

[13] The field police of the German Army, the *feldgendarmerie*, were easily distinguished because of the crescent-shaped metal gorget which they wore while on duty, suspended by a metal chain around the neck.

[14] The *Prosper réseau* (which took its name from the field name of its principal organizer, Francis Suttill) was a resistance network covering a wide swathe of northern France. Some of the reasons why it was disastrously compromised and virtually destroyed in 1943 have long been known beyond dispute. But the full story may never be known and has been the subject of controversy for decades. If Pickersgill and Macalister had been successful in the mission they had been given of forming a new network centred on Sedan in north-eastern France, it would have been a sub-circuit of the *Prosper* network.

[15] In December 1588, the Duc de Guise and his brother, the Cardinal de Guise, after ascending the celebrated spiral stairway of the Château of Blois to attend a meeting in the Council Chamber to which they had been treacherously summoned by Henry III, were seized by the King's bodyguard and murdered.

[16] Rawicz, where Macalister is believed to have been imprisoned — along with Pickersgill — from October 1943 until March 1944, is located in Poland between Poznan and Wroclaw, close to the pre-1939 border between Poland and Germany.

[17] During the Nazi regime, inmates of the prison at Rawicz who were under interrogation or who were considered to be particularly dangerous were held in solitary confinement. A daily work quota was set for all such prisoners.

[18] The journey from Paris to Buchenwald is described in detail in *The White Rabbit* by Bruce Marshall "from the story told him by Wing Commander F.F.E. Yeo-Thomas." As the senior officer, Yeo-Thomas assumed command of the group of Allied agents on the transport, which included Pickersgill and Macalister.

[19] In the apse of the Roman Catholic Church of Mary the Immaculate in Guelph, there is a marble replica of the great *pietà* by Michelangelo in St. Peter's in Rome.

[20] The Buchenwald concentration camp was constructed in 1937 on the south slope of the Ettersberg, a hill some five miles to the northwest of Weimar.

[21] Although the film made, on Hitler's orders, of the execution in Plötzenzee prison of many of the conspirators against his life has either disappeared or been destroyed, its existence and what it contained were put beyond doubt after the War by a number of those who had seen it, including Albert Speer, as well as by the photographer himself. See Peter Hoffmann, *The History of the German Resistance 1939–1945*, p. 719.

JOHN
KENNETH
MACALISTER

DOUGLAS
LEPAN

Acknowledgements

This is a work of fiction, of imagination. But it is based on all the facts
...nd death that I have been able to ascertain
...espondence, archival enquiries, and published
... been made much more difficult because
...hild, and on his parents' death the family
...n either destroyed or irreparably dispersed.
...en able to find any family letters of the kind
...rge H. Ford's two valuable books about

... fortunate enough to be given access to an
...ister's letters which are held in the archives of
...nd which throw light on several crucial
...or giving me access to these papers and
...opies I am indebted to the present Warden of
...y Kenny, and his very helpful secretaries.
...ve are now held by the Foreign and
...Whitehall, under the supervision of Gervase
...ovided me with copies of the reports made
... in training as a secret agent and also of the
...pectively on Pickersgill and Macalister's
abortive mission to France. I am indebted to Mr. Cowell not only for
these courtesies but also for his always sympathetic understanding of
what I have been endeavouring to do. I should also mention that it was
David Stafford who first recommended that I seek Mr. Cowell's
assistance.

For information about Macalister's life in Canada, both in

Guelph and in Toronto at University College, I have to thank George Penfold, Mary (Paddison) Scott, George Hindley, and Charles Crenna (all of whom attended the Guelph Collegiate and Vocational Institute at the same time as he did); together with Eugene Durrant, who taught there; Hazel Burrows, who lived in the house next to his; Abraham Acker, his family's lawyer; and William Beattie and Eric Yarrill, who both lived in the University College Men's Residence at 73 St. George Street during his years there. It was Mr. Penfold who took the initiative in raising money to establish a scholarship in his memory at GCVI in 1977 and who, as part of that initiative, began collecting information about him. Both Mr. Penfold and Mrs. Scott have been generous in sharing this material with me, including very interesting memoranda drawn up by the Hon. J. W. Pickersgill, Frank's elder brother, and by the late Alison (Grant) Ignatieff, who knew them both well in London during the War.

Of cardinal importance in trying to picture Macalister after he enlisted in the British Army in 1940 are letters I have had from Francis Cammaerts and the late Harry Rée. For a few months at the end of 1942, he was Francis Cammaerts' conducting officer; and earlier he and Harry Rée had served as sergeants together in the same small detail of a Field Security Section. I have also had the advantage of correspondence with Peter Lee, who was his commanding officer while he was serving in Field Security Sections attached to SOE; of conversations with Kay (Moore) Gimpel, who also knew him well in London during the War; and of correspondence with Henry Probert, whose home in Cheshire he often visited.

The published literature about SOE is now very extensive. And, of course, the literature about Buchenwald and the network of Nazi concentration camps of which it was a part is much greater still. All I can do is to draw attention to a few books which I have found particularly helpful. M.R.D. Foot's official history of *SOE in France* is still basic and indispensable. In addition, I am indebted to him for several very informative letters and for a very informative interview over lunch in London in the fall of 1991. It was at much the same time that I had the pleasure of a long and highly interesting interview with Vera Atkins, who played such an important role in F section of SOE.

Other books that I must mention are *Solitary Confinement* and *The Dungeon Democracy*, both by Christopher Burney; *"Jacqueline"* by Stella King; *A Quiet Courage* by Liane Jones; *Canadians Behind Enemy Lines* by Roy MacLaren; *All the King's Men* by Robert Marshall; and *The White Rabbit* by Bruce Marshall ("from the story told him by Wing Commander F. F. E. Yeo-Thomas"). To supplement what Yeo-Thomas has to say in *The White Rabbit* about Pickersgill and Macalister, I am indebted to Jack H. Yocom for letting me see an unpublished letter from Yeo-Thomas that was written in 1952.

In some of the areas covered by the books mentioned above I have been the beneficiary of special help and special tuition. I think, first, of parachuting and of the help I have received from Ray Wooler, a Canadian now living in Nova Scotia, who was SOE's principal parachute expert. I am also indebted to Alan Hewitt of Toronto for sharing with me his recollections of serving as a despatcher with the Special Duties Squadrons that dropped parachutists into Europe.

Even those most expert in the history of SOE seem to know little about the prison at Rawicz in Poland. But, by good luck, I was directed by a visiting scholar at Massey College to a book about it in Polish, which I found very helpful and which was translated for me by Piotr Zembrowski.

When I visited Dhuizon in the Sologne in the fall of 1991, I found that what had happened there on the 21st of June 1943 was still vivid in the minds of many of the villagers. For obtaining detailed information for me about it, I am indebted to the present Maire, Pierre Foucher; to Henri Dedun; and particularly to Pierre Hahusseau, who prepared for me a long memorandum which included the evidence of a number of witnesses who still survive and who were present when Pickersgill and Macalister were brought to the Mairie for interrogation. My gratitude to him is profound.

I hope that the epigraph to this book will at least hint at my indebtedness to Primo Levi. But I welcome this opportunity to make explicit my admiration for him both as a man and a writer, and to acknowledge how deeply my own views have been affected by what he has written about the concentration camps and about the Holocaust.

It is with her permission that this book is dedicated to Madame Jeannine Macalister. I am grateful to her for that, but also for talking with me at length about her husband and for providing me with copies of letters about him.

In the various stages of revision I have benefited from the helpful comments of Chris Merillat, Jeff Round, Don LePan, Nick Blatchford, Charles Ritchie — and perhaps most of all from the sensitive enthusiasm and understanding of Modris Eksteins.

Finally, I am indebted to Patricia Kennedy, whose impeccable typing has been a constant pleasure and constant encouragement.